ACKNOWLEDGEMENTS

Elizabeth would like to thank Ruben van Leer for his creative genius and the team at CBRE for looking beyond the corporate ceiling to a healthier future.

A special thanks to the brilliant academic team for putting together a difficult but insightful research study. I am thankful for Dr. Matthijs Noordzij's effortless intellect and constant enthusiasm and Dr. Miriam Vollenbroek-Hutten's consistently ingenious and inspiring guidance. I'm also grateful to Dr. Tibert Verhagen, who always sees the future even when it involves me. Thanks for seeing potential in this misfit.

David would like to thank Erika Vargane Kiss for support and inspiration and Bill Procter for providing a much-needed Geordie reality check on occasion

We're both extremely grateful to Marie-Helene Dibenedetto for her support and wise words. Joan Nelson was peerless in her eagle-eyed proofreading and astute observations. Nick White's enthusiasm and input was a constant source of inspiration.

THE HEALTHY OFFICE
REVOLUTION

ABOUT ELIZABETH NELSON

Elizabeth is a researcher and writer fascinated by human behavior. She believes in applying research findings to practice and has committed her career to bridging the gap between academic research and business. Her company Learn Adapt Build (LAB) works with businesses to give them insight and help them transform the way they work.

Find out more about Elizabeth at www.learnadaptbuild.com

ABOUT DAVID HOLZER

David is the author and ghostwriter of 20 books. He is a business writer, blogger, journalist and occasional performance poet. David is also a writing coach and mentor, specializing in teaching the benefits of yoga for writers through online courses, workshops and one-to-one classes.

Find out more about David at www.davidholzer.com.

PART ONE

THE AGENCY

Before I had even told the beautiful receptionist my name, I was already in love with what I'll call The Agency. It was 2006 and I was 23.

After I told her I was Elizabeth Nelson and that I'd come to see John the Chief Operating Officer, I click-clacked across the reception area on the high heels I never normally wore and sank into a vast sofa, the pleather portfolio, holding five copies of my resume, in my lap. I tilted back my head and looked up into the vast atrium. Above a wall of arty black and white photos of people who, I guessed, worked at the agency, were thick raw crisscrossing wooden beams, steel walkways connecting open plan offices, a roof of windows and the Washington State sky.

I still couldn't quite believe I was really at The Agency for a job interview. Like anyone who works in advertising, I knew all about The Agency. It was, and is, one of the world's leading independent advertising agency, with a reputation for being ultra-creative, with offices in all the world's capitals of cool. Whenever I saw a great commercial on TV, magazine ad or whatever, it nearly always turned out to have been done by The Agency. It was as different from the small Denver advertising agency specializing in real estate where I worked as a research assistant as you could get.

After only a few months at the Denver agency I'd started to go slightly insane with boredom and frustration. I started to explore my possibilities, was incredibly lucky and managed to get my foot in the door of The Agency through the dad of a friend of mine. He was the financial advisor to the CEO. I had to push my friend to the point where I knew our friendship was strained to the limit but she finally told me that her dad had asked the CEO to give me a break. He'd spoken to John, and an interview of sorts was arranged for me.

As I sat in the sofa, trying not to be swallowed alive, I watched the people in the atrium photos stride past me. They were all tall and thin and radiated health and confidence in perfectly fitting jeans and just-so sneakers. To me, they were already gods or superheroes. I realized my cheap suit had been a terrible mistake. Half an hour or so later I was taken to meet John. Unlike the young warriors I'd seen striding through the reception area, John was conservatively dressed in a blue button-down suit and chinos. The smile on his pink, perfectly shaved face was amused and tolerant. Which meant I was more than a little startled when, without even glancing at the resume I'd handed him, John leant forward, looked me in the eye and said, "What's the craziest thing you've ever done?"

I was stumped for a second and then remembered something. I took a deep breath. "When I was doing my bachelor's degree in business with a minor in economics, I went on a class trip to visit the great museums in Rome, Venice, and Florence. Florence blew me away and I decided I had to go to art school there. I managed to persuade my professors to take the necessary classes, which wasn't easy."

John shifted in his seat and nodded for me to go on.

"I hadn't done art in ages so I borrowed a friend's key to the art building and worked on putting my portfolio together at night. I submitted my work to the international office at the very last minute and prayed I'd done enough to be accepted."

"And did you?"

I smiled. "Six months later I was knee-deep in canvases, cappuccinos and a green-eyed Sicilian I met in my first week in Florence. I decided to forget everything I thought I knew and embrace my incredible adventure, like I did on the back of my Sicilian's motorcycle as we roared up the hills just outside Florence, heading to his favorite spot. When we paused for a break between kisses, I asked him who lived behind the huge gate we were parked in front of. 'Papa,' he said, 'the Pope. It's his summer house.' He shrugged. 'But it's OK. He's not here now.' And that's it," I said. "The craziest thing I've ever done. So far."

"Bravo," John said, clapping his hands. "I think you'd be perfect here."

John made an appointment for me to talk with Kelly, The Agency's recruiter, the next morning. He shook my hand, chuckled, shook his head and said "You surprised me, Liz. I didn't see that story coming. Good for you. You're a brave girl. And the best of luck with Kelly. I'm rooting for you."

I was on such a high as I floated out of John's office, down through The Agency and out onto the street. I spent that night tucked away in the corner of a bar in the hip Capitol Hill area of Seattle people watching, sipping a dark craft beer and trying to look as much like I belonged as I could before heading back to my hotel for an early night.

I needed to be fresh and ready for anything my new life was going to throw at me.

Kelly was a sharp-faced woman a little older than me. Although I was careful to mask my bubbling excitement with a veneer of professional cool, she made me feel like a child. She opened our conversation by raising an eyebrow when she saw the age on my resume. Not only that, I didn't have enough experience and lived out of state. I took huge pleasure in telling her "Oh really, John thought I would be a great fit for one of the new accounts The Agency's just won." These were a soda, coffee company, and a brand of men's toiletries.

After Kelly composed her face, she arranged meetings for me with all of The Agency's account directors the next day. The meetings took eight hours and the day was like an endurance test. I wasn't given a single glass of water, not even when I had an interview with the account director of The Agency's enormous soda account who had a huge glass-fronted fridge in her workspace. Despite this, I felt like I made a good impression.

When the ordeal was over, I met with Kelly again.

"You did great, Liz," Kelly said. "But," she paused and I took a large gulp of water, "we have a problem."

"Which is?"

"You live out of state and we don't pay moving costs for juniors."

"What does that mean?" I asked the question as politely as I could.

"It means that if you want to work here you'll have to pay your own moving costs."

"So, if I move to Seattle I can have a job?"

"No. You have a lot of competition and by the time you get here they could have someone in Seattle who could start right away. The Agency moves fast. Just saying."

As soon as Kelly told me that, I was even more determined to move to Seattle and become part of The Agency. I pictured myself bumping into Kelly in a corridor when I was on my way to a vitally important meeting, greeting her with a big "Hi. Can't stop!" and hurrying off before she had a chance to say anything.

I gave her my best big smile, shook her hand and said, "I'll be in touch."

After just the briefest taste of The Agency, there was just no way I could settle back in Denver. My work seemed silly and pointless. I went from loving the city where I'd gone to school and where two of my brothers lived to feeling trapped overnight. I just knew my real life was going on somewhere else.

It took a week before I decided to act on what I knew in my heart I really wanted to do. I handed in my notice at the real estate ad agency, gave up the lease on my apartment and, through Craigslist, paid a shockingly expensive deposit and my first and last month's rent in advance on a place in Seattle, which I would be sharing with three other girls.

Three weeks later, I headed west on I-80 with my brother and a friend of his in the friend's van. I drove behind in my Toyota corolla. It was only a 20-hour road trip but, as we headed up through Idaho and Oregon to Washington State, we treated it like an epic adventure. Little sister was going west to a new life.

It took three weeks of calling Kelly before I finally got ahold of her. She told me she'd left The Agency, making it sound like her choice. I insisted she meet me for coffee. When we met in a Starbucks she looked pale and deflated, reinforcing my belief that she hadn't left The Agency but had been pushed out for some reason. Although I'd moved out to Seattle on her advice, I felt sorry for her. I had my dream to chase. Hers had been taken away from her.

Kelly sighed and said "I'm impressed, Liz. I didn't think you had it in you to move to Seattle without a safety net. But there really isn't anything I can do. I wish there was. I feel for you. As far as I know they're not hiring at the moment but here's the name of the new recruiter." She wrote the name down on a scrap of paper for me and I immediately put it in my phone contacts list.

Heading back to Denver with my tail between my legs wasn't an option. There was nothing for me there, anyway. To cover the cost of living in the city, which wasn't cheap, I worked two jobs. One was in an art gallery that belonged to a friend of a friend from Minnesota. It took me a long time to be able to eat an hors d'oeuvre after that. My other job was at a restaurant. At least I didn't starve. But I had no life.

I didn't give up hope of being allowed into the hallowed halls of The Agency but I came close. Whenever my faith did wobble, I thought of that little real estate ad agency in Denver and shuddered.

I kept emailing the recruiter at The Agency and stopped by with quirky little presents like fancy cupcakes from an artisan bakery downtown or silly cards for her. It took a month but I finally got a reply telling me there was a temporary position in the creative recruiting department. One and a half hours after I opened the email I was invited for an interview with Brook.

Waiting in The Agency reception area, I did my best not to let my hopes soar to the roof of the atrium. Thinking back, this probably helped because I came across as cool, calm, and collected when I was actually already resigned to the possibility of disappointment. I told myself that, whatever happened, I wouldn't have failed. It wasn't much consolation.

Brook turned out to be a tall, elegant woman with long blonde hair expensively styled to look natural. She looked like a model and turned out to have been a quite successful one back in the day. I was ready to be intimidated by her but she put me at ease with a smile so big it made her eyes crinkle up in the sweetest way. We shook hands and she suggested we talk outside on the deck.

The deck was bigger than my entire apartment and we sat on two chairs that must have cost more than all my furniture. "I'm impressed by your perseverance, Liz," Brook said. "Why do you want to work here so much?"

I took a deep breath and decided to tell the truth.

———◆———

My first day at The Agency began with me trailing around after Brook as she introduced me to all the beautiful, creative people. According to Brook, I was "fantastic, brilliant, going places, the next big thing." As she told my new colleagues to "Watch this girl," I wished they wouldn't.

I stayed quiet and smiled. Thinking about it now, this might have been the beginning of me being labeled "too nice for advertising." My outfit probably didn't help. I wore a sundress and a blazer. This wasn't really my style but it was the only outfit in my closet that was cute and professional and wasn't a suit. The looks I got from some of the other girls let me know I was still overdressed.

After Brook had introduced and embarrassed me, I settled down at my gorgeous rustic wood desk, moved the mouse of my Apple computer and watched the huge screen come to life. If anyone had asked me a question at that moment I wouldn't have been able to answer. I was so happy. It felt like I was home, among my people. At last.

On my first day, I hadn't thought to bring any food with me and I wasn't sure about the protocol. I also didn't have much money. By the time Brook invited me to eat with her and her agency friends at a nearby restaurant I was ravenous. I said as little as possible throughout the meal and concentrated on not spilling my soup.

Brook's agency friends were slightly more awkward clones of her. They were x-ray thin but, as I found out at lunch, they all ate and ate. Everyone talked about work, which was okay with me because I wanted to find out as much as I could. This was my introduction to the fact that 99.9% of all conversations at The Agency were work-related. For the people who worked on the massive sportswear account, even talking about whether the Seahawks were going to beat the 49ers was part of the job.

If they weren't talking about work, the girls were swapping tips on which drugs worked best for which viruses. Although they looked amazing, they all seemed to be ill. I guessed that being at work while you were nursing a terrible cold was a badge of honor. I felt great.

Brook gave me my first assignment that afternoon. I was to look for the best talent in advertising—the most creative designers, art directors and copywriters—see who was winning awards, being talked about in magazine articles, make a note of their names and put together files on rising stars. I'd gotten a passion for research in school and at my last agency and discovered I had a talent for it so I quickly became engrossed in my detective work.

Outstanding creatives, as they're called, are the lifeblood of any good agency. At The Agency, which prided and sold itself on the creativity of its ad campaigns, creatives were truly prized and nurtured. This was a philosophy or strategy that meant The Agency was voted most creative agency of the year several years running.

The Agency also had a way of bringing out the best in people that seemed counterintuitive at first but which, I came to realize, made total sense. Art directors—the people who did the visual side of things in ads and commercials—would be paired off with copywriters whose track record and approach was completely different. A male copywriter who had worked on, let's say, beer, would be partnered with a female with a portfolio of work relating to apparel. They would then be put to work on a children's toy account. Catapulting creatives out of their comfort zone would often result in work that really pushed the boundaries.

I would learn that creative work came first and the client, or "the man" as they were called, came a distant second.

I nearly jumped out of my skin when Brook said, "It's 5.30, Liz time to go home. What will people say about me if they see you here this late? Don't be like me, go home, have a life."

I laughed but said "It's okay, I'd like to stay." I wanted to look committed and to find out what the office was like after dark. The truth was I also had nowhere else to be.

My roommates were not much more than vaguely friendly ghostly presences to me. Rita was a first-generation Indian girl who I could tell was far smarter than she liked to appear. She had a pet bunny rabbit that wasn't technically allowed in the apartment but which hopped around like it owned the place. Different as we were, I got the feeling Rita and I could be friends. Tara worked in a bar and dated a guy who worked on The Agency's sports brand account. She was always talking about "The Agency this, The Agency that," bathing in his reflected glory. I thought about asking her to put in a good word with him for me but something told me this would be a bad idea. Sam was hardly ever home and when she was, her door was kept firmly closed until she re-emerged bursting with energy, blue hair teased to towering heights, her make up done to show off her big, slightly crazy, eyes and wearing the strangest juxtaposition of clothes I'd ever seen. She thought nothing of wearing an old lady's jacket, purple vinyl pants and retro sandals with clear plastic heels.

In their own ways, these three were about as different from me, a Midwestern girl from Saint Paul, Minnesota as they could possibly be. I was as blonde as Sam was blue, thanks to my Swedish roots. But, in my quiet way, I was just as up for an adventure.

I didn't regard the people I worked with at the gallery and restaurant as real friend material. Sitting in bars by myself had gotten old very quickly. There were some beautiful places to walk and run in Seattle but having two jobs had kept me so exhausted I'd stopped running. Walking in the park without a boyfriend or dog made me feel like a total loser.

"Suit yourself, Liz," Brook said as she put on an immaculately battered biker jacket. "But, be careful, staying late can become an addiction. I'm out of here."

I was amazed by what I saw next. Orders of pizza, sushi and salads began being delivered to the office around six and didn't stop until I left at midnight. Some people who I guessed had families left by eight, which left only single people alone and unsupervised in what I soon realized was more like a play-ground than an office.

By the time I finally left for the evening, I'd seen another side of paradise. Although they were still working, people relaxed, turned the music up a little, munched on snacks and started to flirt with each other. I loved it.

———————◆———————

For those first few weeks all I did was find my feet. I started leaving home 30 minutes early in the morning just to make sure I found my way to the right room in The Agency building. Another reason for getting up earlier was to work on my makeup and do my best to look like Brook and the other beautiful, stylish giraffes that inhabited The Agency. The thing about Brook was, although she still had her model's figure and wore tight jeans and rock and roll t-shirts to show it off, there was nothing girly about her. Perhaps because she still carried herself like a model, Brook's height added to her presence.

I did my best not to make it look like I was copying Brook but I raised my game and invested in some cute and expensive blouses, jackets, and high heels for work only. I wasn't yet ready to bring my own leather jacket, white t-shirts, jeans and motor-cycle boots into work.

The pressure to look as great as I could didn't stop me from adoring Brook. She was everyone at The Agency's favorite person and one of the major reasons so many people applied to join us. She totally got the importance of creatives to The Agency and seemed to genuinely adore them herself. Whether she did or not, Brook had the knack of appearing to empathize with anyone. Her technique was to look them straight in the eye, nod a lot and say "Yes!" whenever it seemed like the conversation needed it.

This is not to say that Brook was ever fake. Far from it. I never saw her be anything but sincere and decent. It was just that although she was friends with everyone at The Agency, she never seemed to really let her guard down. I wasn't sure if this was a technique she'd learned or if it was part of a natural reserve.

Brook would go to the Cannes Lions International Festival of Advertising and come back with the top creatives in the business begging her to call them. They would fall over themselves to move to Seattle from the East Coast, South America, Asia, and Europe. She repaid their commitment to her with absolute loyalty.

———◆———

One afternoon I almost took out at least 15 people as I ran across the building with a set of portfolios. I wanted to get them to Brook, who was in a meeting that was running late, so she could take them on to her next one. My plan was to be waiting for her when she got out of the meeting, making it look like I'd been waiting for a while.

I stood outside the meeting room catching my breath. After a minute or so I began to feel like I was being watched. I turned around and locked eyes with a guy in his late thirties, maybe even early forties. He was gorgeous, wearing a designer t-shirt and jeans that made him look better than most men would have in a tux. Leaning against one of the wooden beams, he looked me up and down slowly, smiling the whole time. I smiled back and took a deep breath, hoping to calm my racing heart.

Brook strode out of the meeting room, took the proofs from me and was about to head off when she saw the guy looking at me. "Oh, hi Sean," she said. "Have you met my new assistant Liz?"

"No," Sean said. "Hello Liz." I smiled and waved.

Raising his eyebrow as if he found my awkwardness simply fascinating, Sean turned to walk away. Without looking back he said "Welcome to The Agency. See ya around."

Sitting at my desk later that afternoon I was deeply confused and counting the seconds until the day was over. I wanted to run home and try to make sense of what had happened, as well as why I was so disturbed by Sean. Instead, some of the commercial producers, girls who sat near me, invited me to have a drink at the local bar.

This was technically part of The Agency building but, because you had to take four steps to reach the door, it felt a little like you were going somewhere. I hadn't been inside yet. Just walking past and gazing in through the window at the chic interior made me feel like I was spending the little money I had. That afternoon I'd helped myself to some extra pizza on the second floor at around four so I didn't have to buy food and had enough money for a couple of overpriced drinks without jeopardizing my ability to pay my rent.

Being with the girls was so much fun. They overflowed with stories of the latest commercial shoots they'd been on and what the professional athletes and actors they worked with were really like. I sipped my drink, listened and giggled until one of the girls turned to me and said "What about you, Liz?"

I gulped. "Um, wow, I can't really compete with any of those stories."

The girl laughed. "No, I mean how's it going so far. Who are you working with? And, most important, who do you think is cute?"

"Who me?" I stammered. "I'm working with Brook in creative recruiting, um…"

"We know," she said, pantomiming a yawn but laughing. "So tell us who you like in The Agency or at least who you've noticed."

"I haven't really noticed anyone." She looked disappointed. They all did. I felt like I'd ruined their evening. The stories they told, the gossip they were dishing, were incredible and I couldn't compete. Also, I knew that if you don't dish back it sends a message that you can't be trusted. I tried to think of something but all I could come up with was the story of my encounter with Sean.

"Actually, there was this weird thing that happened today," I said. The girl waited, her eyes sparkling. "I had to drop off some stuff for Brook today, portfolios and proofs, and there was this guy. I think he was a creative. And, well, he looked at me."

Her nose wrinkled. "He, like, looked at you?"

"He really looked at me. He wouldn't stop. Like he was analyzing me or memorizing every detail about me or something."

They all started to laugh. "Oh god, which creative was it I wonder?"

"Art directors are so intense," another girl said. "The vampires of the creative world. Driven by lust and chasing absolute perfection and beauty. Sarah just broke up with one on the soda account."

"You don't break up with a creative," Sarah said. "You detox from them. There are normal, nice creatives in other agencies but not here. Out of curiosity, did he, um, have a name?"

"Sean," I said.

There was a long silence and Sarah said "Ah, take your time. Don't hook up with anyone for the first month. Until you know your way around. You wouldn't want to make any terrible mistakes."

One of the girls changed the subject to an after party some of them had been to the week before. I was surprised by their reaction to my news but didn't want to make waves. I tried to follow the conversation and be interesting enough to be invited for drinks again.

We finished around midnight. I paid the 50 bucks for my three drinks—a fortune to me—and went back to the office to get my coat and bag. Brook sat at her desk, gazing at her computer, a glass of wine in her hand. Her coat was wrapped around her shoulders, her eyes and nose were red and her skin was blotchy. She looked exhausted.

"Are you all right?" I said, immediately conscious of the effect of three drinks on my voice.

"Yeah," she said. "But I've had a bad cold or flu or something for a couple weeks now. I take a few Dayquil to get me through work and some glorious Nyquil to put me in a small coma every night. I'll shake it eventually but for now it's fine."

I couldn't imagine being sick for two weeks straight and working through it. Maybe it was just good genes or my obsession with staying healthy but I couldn't remember the last time I'd been sick.

Grabbing my stuff, I said goodnight and headed out the door. I decided to walk home to clear my head. I thought about the girls' reaction to my news about Sean. Had I said something wrong? Was he dating one of the girls? Was he a player? I really hoped I hadn't blown my chances with the girls. I'd been in Seattle for a month now and hadn't met anyone outside the office.

But I had to admit to myself that I'd loved the way Sean stared at me.

The first thing I heard next morning when I arrived at work even earlier than usual was a boisterous "Good morning!" from Brook.

She was already at her desk and one-finger typing at an incredible speed. In her free hand she held a Starbucks cup the size of a flower vase. She looked amazing, the picture of health. I listened as she gave me that day's schedule and told me what I needed to do.

"I can't believe how good you look," I said finally.

"Thank you," Brook said. "I had the most delicious coma last night. This morning I took a Dayquil and today I'm Wonder Woman again."

I couldn't keep the surprise off my face. I thought she'd been joking about the Dayquil and Nyquil. "Don't look so shocked, Liz," she said. "Your generation uses Adderall in these situations, right?" She nudged me. "Do you have any, by the way?"

When I shook my head, Brook looked disappointed for a second but shrugged her shoulders. "Oh well," she said, "let's grab these portfolios and set them up in my room for my ten o'clock."

We were bent over the portfolios when something made me look up. Sean was standing behind Brook, staring into my eyes, a half-smile on his lips. "Um, Brook," I said.

"What?"

"Sean is here to see you."

Brook straightened up, looked at me, raised an eyebrow and turned around to face Sean. "Yes, Sean," she said. "What can I do for you?"

"I, ah, I'd like another art director for my team," Sean said.

"Really? What happened to Stacey?"

"Oh, she's great. I just feel like we could do with someone who, you know..."

"I think I do, Sean. When do you need this new art director by?"

"No rush. I just, you know, wanted to get things moving. Give you a heads-up."

"Thank you, Sean. I appreciate it. Now, you'll have to excuse Liz and me. We were due at our meeting five minutes ago."

"Of course. See you around." Sean made a funny little bow which I have to say I thought was charming.

When he'd gone, Brook said. "Watch that one, Liz."

Love isn't in the air

A couple of months passed and I began to feel like I was settling in at The Agency. Or I just about lost the feeling that I was going to be revealed as an imposter at any minute and asked to leave. In those early days, I would have been heartbroken to leave The Agency. To be honest, if it had happened, I would probably still be devastated now.

This was simply the most stimulating environment I'd ever been in. I was addicted to the energy I could feel in the air. The creatives were so full of ideas that time, hunger and sleep were suspended. Production people buzzed on adrenalin as they fixed all kinds of last-minute glitches and met impossible deadlines 24/7. And, drifting through the madness with Zen composure, the account director.

All this energy was grounded in a will that had taken The Agency to the heights of the world of advertising. The huge wooden beams, steel surrounds and vast expanses of raw concrete made an undeniable statement of pure strength. Every morning when I walked in through eighteen-foot high doors and said "Hi" to the receptionist, whose beauty and composure never failed to amaze me, I couldn't stop myself from looking up into the atrium and marveling at the place.

I felt bigger, more impressive as a person. I felt comfortable and secure. All my worries and "what-ifs?" were wiped from my brain. At only twenty-three I was working at the greatest place I could have imagined. I had already made something of myself, proof to everyone that I was at the beginning of an amazing career.

I still remember the first time I was wandering home past a store in Seattle and saw a poster campaign I'd first glimpsed as an example of The Agency's latest award-winning work high up on those raw concrete walls. I was so thrilled.

When I called my mom back home in Saint Paul, I would tell her to look out for the TV commercials produced by The Agency. I adored the feeling that I knew what was really going on, that I breathed the same air as the geniuses who shaped the way America behaved. I was an insider!

One night we were talking on the phone, each sipping a glass of wine. I had grown to love these moments with my mom. I was old enough and stable enough that we could just talk like friends. "What do you really feel about what I'm doing, Mom?" I asked.

She paused. I heard the sound of wine trickling from a bottle into a glass. "I'm proud of you, and really impressed by the scale of the work you're doing. I mean, you're only twenty-three."

"Buuuut?"

You've always been ambitious and in the past you've been rewarded for your initiative. But business is so political and many people would rather you stroke their ego than do great work. I'm not sure if the people you're working for will really reward you or just expect you to kiss ass. What do you think?"

"I don't know. I hope so. It looks like it."

"Whatever happens, Liz, you're going to learn at least part of it the hard way. We all do. You're ambitious and you're going to find out that ambition is rewarded. But it's also punished."

"What does that mean?"

She sighed. "It can't be explained because the behavior doesn't make any sense. You'll find out, sweetheart, unfortunately. We all do. The hard way. But, right now, just enjoy what you're doing. Remember not to take on too much. You sound so tired when I talk to you. But you sound better now." She sipped her wine. "Any cute guys?"

I squirmed. "Kind of but, you know, I'm still settling in."

"What about that guy, the blind date guy?"

My mom had set up the blind date for me through a friend of a colleague of hers. We had an okay night, drank some local beers and ate appetizers at a cool brewpub called The Ishmael in the Capitol Hill district of Seattle. Let's say we didn't exactly hit it off. He didn't ask to see me again and I was relieved.

"You know, mom. We did the growing up in Minnesota thing for a bit then ran out of stuff to talk about. He was a nice guy though so it was probably me.

But don't worry about me, I'm fine."

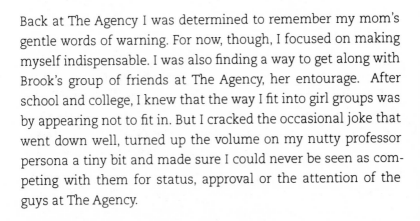

Back at The Agency I was determined to remember my mom's gentle words of warning. For now, though, I focused on making myself indispensable. I was also finding a way to get along with Brook's group of friends at The Agency, her entourage. After school and college, I knew that the way I fit into girl groups was by appearing not to fit in. But I cracked the occasional joke that went down well, turned up the volume on my nutty professor persona a tiny bit and made sure I could never be seen as competing with them for status, approval or the attention of the guys at The Agency.

My slight oddness was for the time being my greatest strength. That, and my work ethic. They disguised it well but it didn't take long before I realized that the entourage all looked up to Brook. They dressed like her in clothes that were every bit as expensively down-market—wearing any kind of fashionable label was seen as trying too hard—but they never quite nailed her look. I also got used to what I called Brookisms. One girl would say "As Brook says...," another would say "I was talking to Brook the other day and..." Because Brook was my immediate boss, I had plenty of opportunity to dispense Brookisms but I did try to catch myself if I heard the same phrase coming out of my mouth more than a couple of times.

At this time, I was painfully aware that I only had a month of my three-month trial to go and didn't have a particularly defined role at The Agency. I had no idea if I was going to be kept on or not. Brook wasn't worried, but then I hadn't seen her worried about anything yet. Still, I was determined to make myself indispensable. I did what Brook asked of me to the best of my ability, whether it was getting the kind of coffee she liked or trying to second-guess what she was really after in a briefing meeting. That being said, Brook never let me get her coffee; it was only if I was going and other people wanted a cup as well, or sometimes I brought her one without asking.

Brook kept me busy. But one afternoon, I had time on my hands and was reorganizing my filing cabinet. I happened to look up when a copywriter and a girl I recognized from production walked past deep in conversation. I thought they were talking about work until I saw their hands brush in a way that looked like it was accidental but which was clearly intentional. I could feel the electricity from where I was standing. I couldn't help but gaze at them as they wandered away down the office until I realized what I was doing, blushed and looked around to see if anyone else had noticed.

It hit me that I hadn't really thought about dating in months. I'd moved to Seattle and The Agency for work and still didn't know anyone. My roommates had their own lives. A couple of times I'd suggested to Rita, who I felt I had most friend potential with, that we go out for a drink together but she'd politely declined. The second time her excuses were so lame I decided not to bother again. You already know about the disastrous blind date.

Standing there, at my filing cabinet, I wondered who my boyfriend might be. I wanted him to be from The Agency, of course. But would he be one of the creatives, who were usually intense and frighteningly quick witted or would he be an ultra-competent commercials producer, a cool, calm and collected account director or an amazingly professional project manager? I forced myself not to think about the mysterious Sean, who I hadn't seen since he'd come to Brook asking for a new art director.

A couple of times I thought I felt him watching me but when I looked over to where I thought he was, it seemed like I'd been mistaken.

———◆———

In my fantasies I would go on a double-date with Brook and her guy who, although I hadn't met him, I was sure would be incredible, and my guy. It would be happy hour and we would share orders of crab cakes, mini sliders and sushi, washed down with good Colombia Valley Cabernet Sauvignon. My guy would be a little nervous but mostly funny and charming. He'd be different enough to find my quirkiness relatively normal. He'd be attractive in an effortless kind of way. I'd once dated a guy who spent a ton of time and product on his hair. Never again.

My guy would be as ambitious as me, and would ideally want to go to Europe as much as I did. Ever since my time in Italy I was determined to go back. He would be a great guy but also wouldn't be too clean-cut or simple. Not that there's anything wrong with that. I had been categorized and simplified my whole life and I was drawn to guys who were decent but exciting. You could clearly see there was something different about them. I didn't want to be a nice Midwestern couple. I wanted someone that would surprise Brook a little; like I constantly hoped I would. She thought of me as sweet, but semi-odd. She roared with laughter when she heard me call a vagina a woman's "lady". So I wanted to impress her.

After our double-date, we'd head off to an Agency party. These were always way more fun than any non-agency party. We were all invited to an amazing event every couple of weeks. The best one I'd been to, given by The Agency, was their Founder's Day party, which took place not long after I joined, and blew my mind. The Agency rented out an entire carnival—a hip version, of course, with contortionists, burlesque dancers and a girl covered with tattoos who swallowed a sword. Gymnasts swung on silk sheets high above fire dancers. Prince played and it was thrilling to see him up close as he worked the tiny, by his standards, stage and dragged every dance move we'd ever known out of us all. By the end of the night I was on a natural high. When one of the single guys on the hot list came up to me and asked where one of the girls in Brook's entourage was I was surprised but not at all disappointed.

"A penny for your thoughts?" Brook's voice cut into my delicious daydream. I blushed like a teenager who'd been caught out. I'd been doing a lot of that since I'd been at The Agency.

"Oh, nothing. I just zoned out for a while." The minute the words were out of my mouth I wished I'd said that I had a fantastic idea for something or other. But, I knew Brook would have called me out. She understood people better than anyone I'd ever met. That both impressed and scared me. And one of the great things about working for Brook was feeling that I could be honest with her, without her judging me.

"I have a meeting in five and I'd like you to sit in on it, if that's okay for you."

"Sure, I'd love to. No problem. Can I get you anything?"

"No, you're fine. Five minutes then."

Brook disappeared in the direction of her desk, leaving me no closer to meeting Mr. Wonderful. But hoping, hoping.

Running scared

I'd soon realized that although people ate at weird hours, usually at their desks, what they actually ate was pretty healthy. There was a Whole Foods grocery store across the street, which in theory made it easy. The problem was that there was a reason why the store was nicknamed Whole Paycheck. I was still finding my feet so I struggled to eat well. There was often free pizza laying around, which made it even harder to resist temptation.

Even though I never saw anyone drink during the day, there were also beer kegs on each corner of every floor. We'd have a beer or two when we were working late but I never saw anyone out of control at work. People would have wine with dinner at the restaurant that functioned almost as The Agency's dining room but they'd often go back to work.

Eating at strange hours, snacking on all that carbohydrate, fat and salt saturated food and being surrounded by all these tall, model-skinny girls began to make me feel out of shape. Back in Denver I'd always made sure I worked out two or three times a week. Since I'd arrived in Seattle, exercise had gone out the window. I felt like I was turning into a whale and my round Midwestern Swedish face was becoming moon-sized.

At lunchtime one day I noticed one of the girls in production slip a lululemon yoga mat and a chic gym bag from under her desk. I watched as she went into one of the bathrooms and came out in a pair of stretch yoga pants and top that showed off her lightly tanned, toned and long-muscled body. Making sure she didn't see me, I followed her to the glass-sided, open-topped fitness area I'd been shown by Brook on my first tour of The Agency but never used. I loved the look of the workout space from the very beginning and thought it was awesome to have such a cool place to work out for free. But I hadn't liked the idea that people could look down on me while training from the upper levels of the building. I'd also been a bit confused about when was a good time to work out. I couldn't imagine that it would look good to leave my desk in the middle of the day and exercise.

Brook always had lots of workout clothes with her but I never saw her work out. Did she work out in the mornings or at night?

Now, I realized I couldn't afford to be shy if I was going to rescue my fitness before I became too much of a slob. And if the yoga girl could take a break to practice I thought I could too.

In the middle of the workout space was a half basketball court where the yoga and fitness classes were held several times a day. Off to the side was a workout room with all the latest machines and TVs with every channel. This is where the girl from production headed. I watched as she joined a group of other girls and a couple of guys preparing for what turned out to be a pretty challenging Vinyasa yoga class.

My first thought was if she could take time out to exercise in the middle of the day so could I. But caution won out and I decided I'd work out first thing in the morning, before my actual work started.

That night I bought a new pair of running shoes and picked out my best workout gear ready for the morning. When I stepped out onto the treadmill I was excited and nervous, determined to show I belonged in the fitness area.

I warmed up, found some music on my iPod, and slipped in the earbuds. I'd found some music in The Agency's library. It had an impressive selection as the "librarian" was also head of sound for the agency. I found an amazing French Canadian group I had seen in concert before. Secretly I wanted to make sure that if anyone asked me what I was listening to I would make a good impression.

The only people on the running machines were me and a lean older guy who ran effortlessly at a steady pace. I saw that his screen was turned off and his eyes were fixed on something only he could see. He gave me a little salute as I climbed onto the machine and set my pace. I imagined he was one of the creative geniuses of The Agency, running after an award-winning campaign idea. I loved the idea of that.

I started running at what I thought was about the right pace. Not so slow that I looked like a lightweight and not so fast that I was going to go red in the face, start panting and need to give up.

After ten minutes, I started to relax and really get into my running. I made a vow to run every day. I drifted off in the way that you do when you're running and the endorphins are kicking in. I started to wonder why a workout was called a workout. I decided it was because I was working something out. Perhaps it was what the guy next to me was doing, the guy I'd decided was a creative god. He was working out a concept. But what was I working out? I had no idea. I allowed my mind to go blank and I lost myself in the music.

But then I began to feel like I was being watched. I put it down to my usual self-consciousness until, without making it look too obvious, I glanced up and saw Brook looking down on me from the third floor. I smiled and waved and Brook waved back.

I couldn't help but speed up a little, which made me smile to myself.

———◆———

I pretended to work at my laptop computer as I sipped my smoothie and glowed. I'd forgotten how much I loved running. I was still enjoying my endorphin high when Brook drifted over to my beautiful desk.

"You looked like you were enjoying yourself," Brook said.

"Oh I was," I said. "I'd forgotten just how much I love running. It's such a luxury to be able to exercise at work."

Brook smiled. "We want you to be happy here, and that means being healthy." She turned as if to walk away and said casually, "One thing, though. If you're going to run here you need a different pair of running shoes."

I thought she mean there was something about the running conditions that my shoes weren't suited for. "Really?" I said.

"Yeah," Brook said. "They're the wrong kind. We only ever wear Escalate here, Sweet Liz."

I blushed scarlet. "Oh shi...shoot," I said. "Of course. I'm so, so sorry. It won't happen again."

"Don't worry, Liz," Brook said. "It's not a capital crime. But wearing Escalate helps us understand the brand from the inside out, to live with it. And if we don't have faith in our clients' products, how can we expect consumers to believe the messages we develop? Also, they like to keep us on our toes by dropping in to see us unannounced. Believe me, it happens."

"It won't happen again," I said.

"I know it won't, Liz. And on your way home tonight call in to the Escalate employee store. Show them your ID card for this place and you'll get a discount on new running shoes or anything you want. Okay?"

"Of course," I said.

"Did you keep the receipt for those New Balance you were rocking on the track today? They looked pretty fresh."

I blushed again. "I did."

"Good," Brook said. "We don't want you to waste your money. Oh, and another thing, do you have the number for that writer I asked you about, the one working for Wieden and Kennedy out of Portland that I want to talk to? I tried calling him and the number didn't work. I must have copied it down wrong."

"Sure, I'll get it for you right now," I said.

With that she winked at me, tapped me on the shoulder with the sheaf of papers she was holding and sat down at her desk.

———•———

For the rest of the day my mind kept going back to my mistake. I felt like I should have been smart enough to have realized that The Agency would think this way. But, on the other hand, I didn't know anything about advertising and I wasn't telepathic.

Most of all, I felt like I'd seen behind the glossy façade of The Agency—the bright eyes and the gleaming smile—for the first time. I'd gotten a taste of how the machine really worked. I suppose I wasn't surprised but I didn't like it.

The slightly bitter taste in my mouth stayed with me all day, until I walked into the sportswear store to exchange my New Balance shoes for Escalate and the sales guy put the first ever wearable device I ever saw or touched into my hand.

Being the difference

After my mess up with the running shoes, I took Brook's advice and only wore sportswear made by Escalate, even when I was out for a run at the opposite end of the city from The Agency. No matter how much I wanted to, I rarely found the time to exercise in the gym at work. I worked so late that it was a real struggle to get up in the morning at all, let alone early enough to go to the workout area.

One morning, however, I managed it. I arrived on the treadmill dressed head to toe in Escalate just as Jim, the head of strategy for the Escalate account, was finishing his run. I smiled at him and started to warm up. "Come and see me later," he said. "I may have something for you."

My first impulse was to run for five minutes and then go straight to Jim's workspace to find out what he had for me but I forced myself to run for thirty minutes. The problem was I was so buzzed I ran faster than I ever had before and I think I pulled a muscle. Still, it meant that I had to walk over to Jim's desk very slowly, which I hoped made me look as laidback as he seemed to be.

"Good run, Liz?" he said.

"Great," I said, sipping my smoothie and trying to pretend sweat wasn't trickling down my forehead into my eyes.

"Please, sit down. I haven't seen you running down there before."

"No," I said, lowering myself gently into the chair next to his desk. "I normally run outside after I get home."

"Wow," he said, "that must be pretty late. You're always here when I leave."

"I like to stay in shape," I said, trying not to wince as I crossed my legs.

"Good for you. That's what we like to hear. So, right, I want you to come and work as a creative and planning assistant on the Escalate account, reporting to Richard, our creative director. I don't know exactly what you've been doing for Brook but you're always at your desk in the morning when I get here and you're still at it when I leave so I guess that means you're a hard worker. Brook says you do excellent work for her and she's given me permission to offer you a place on our team. What do you say?"

My first impulse was to leap out of my chair but I simply nodded and said "I'd love to."

"Fantastic. See you here tomorrow morning."

I floated back to what I was already thinking of as my old desk, trying not to limp. Brook was already at her desk. She smiled at me. "You talked to Jim?" she said.

"I did. Thank you."

Brook leant back in her chair and took a sip of her coffee. "For what, Liz? I just told him you were great at what you do and have lots of potential. But he'd already decided he wanted you. You don't need me to help you make a good impression. You know, I really don't think you're aware of how you come across to people. You're obviously smart and very hard-working, which usually means a person's seriously ambitious. And you're modest with it. What's not to like?"

"Thank you," I said, not trusting myself to say any more.

"You're here to succeed, Liz. This may be a fun place to work but really it's all about proving yourself, justifying your existence. You're doing just fine at that. Stay focused, stay hungry—try not to be too nice—and the rest will take care of itself."

I laughed. "I'll try not to be too nice. But it'll be hard. You can take the girl out of Minnesota but… I'll miss working with you." This was true. I was already feeling a little choked up. Brook had been so kind to me.

"Liz, your new desk is literally a 30 second walk away. It's not like we're going to become strangers. Oh, one thing. You know that number you gave me for the guy at Weiden and Kennedy?"

"Yes."

"I hadn't copied it down wrong. You'd given me the wrong number. I found the right one but I got to him too late."

"Oh."

"Yeah. He'd already accepted a position at Mother in LA."

I felt dizzy. "I am so sorry."

"I know you are, Liz. I won't tell you it doesn't matter because it does. But it isn't the end of the world. Just make sure you double-check everything. Jim is nowhere near as easygoing as I am. Now, don't stand there looking like someone just stole your lunch money. I'm really happy for you, Liz."

———————•———————

That night I left at eight. I would have stayed later but I wanted to tell my Mom the good news. I bought a bottle of Prosecco, changed into my Escalate lounge pants and t-shirt, curled up on my bed, popped the cork, poured a glass of Prosecco and dialed my Mom. The call went to voicemail and I felt a little deflated. "Hi Mom," I said. "I've got great news. Call me back."

Now what? I was itching to share my good news but there was no one else I could call who would get what my new job meant to me. I lay on my bed for a while, staring into space, holding the glass of Prosecco on my belly. This was one of the best days of my life and I had no one to talk to.

I'd finished the glass and was about to pour myself another when I heard Rita's door open and close. She began blasting out music, an amazing fusion of dancey trance stuff and what sounded like Indian music. I swung my legs over the side of the bed, grabbed the bottle and knocked on Rita's door.

When she opened the door, her rabbit Stella tucked under one arm, I waggled the bottle and said "I've got nobody to celebrate with."

"It's about time, girl," Rita said. "Come on in."

Rita's room was packed with stuff but tidy. The largest thing in the room was a flat-screen TV, its sound turned down. On it, Indian men and women dressed in costumes so bright they made my eyes ache threw themselves around in a beautiful dance routine.

We'd finished my bottle of Prosecco and were halfway through another which Rita had magically plucked up out of nowhere when my Mom called back. I stepped into the hallway and told her my news. "Sounds like you're having fun, darling. Give me a call tomorrow night. And don't drink too much."

"Mom! I never do."

"Hmmm," she said. "Love you."

"Love you too, Mom."

My phone said the time was eleven. "Time to switch to water," I said. "Big day tomorrow."

"Why?" Rita asked.

It was only then that I realized I hadn't told her what I was celebrating. "I got a new job at The Agency today," I said. "It means I'm permanent."

"Wow, Liz. That's fantastic." We clinked glasses. "What's the job?"

"I'm a creative and planning assistant on probably our biggest account." I pointed at the logo on my chest. "These guys," I said.

"Awesome. What does a creative and planning assistant do?"

I giggled. "Um, I'm not really sure."

"But you'll find out, right?"

"Yep." I stroked the rabbit, which was curled up on my lap. I knew I should go to bed but Rita was the first person I'd had a meaningful conversation with in the whole of Seattle who didn't work for The Agency. I hadn't realized how starved I was for simple girl talk. "What do you do, Rita?"

"I'm a social worker for the government. I'm doing my counseling rotation out of school right now, paying off my student loans. But I'm going to be a counselor. Set up my own practice. It's easier here than New York, where I studied. Cheaper."

"Don't you miss New York?"

"Nah. Not really. Anyway my family's all out in the Bay Area. I'm close enough to them here. And far away enough, if you know what I mean."

"Why do you do what you do?"

Rita raised an eyebrow but she smiled. "Because I want to help people. Like Gandhi is supposed to have said, to 'be the change in the world I wish to see.' Don't you want to change things?"

"Of course."

"So why advertising?"

"I love the way it combines so many great things. Beautiful design, inspiring words and psychology to figure out what makes people tick. Maybe this sounds silly to you but I really think of it as a modern-day form of art. Look at the Escalate commercials.

They're so empowering."

"Maybe," Rita said.

"Okay, my turn," I said. "How do you help people?"

"This is what happened to me today, Liz. I have a new client, a woman. The court has paid for her to have three counseling sessions with me. She's in a custody battle with her husband. He's been beating her for years now and started hitting the kids. She fought back and tried to run away but he called the cops and got her arrested for domestic abuse. She doesn't have any evidence of the beating and doesn't work so the court is thinking of giving him full custody. I'm working on helping her heal emotionally but also coaching her on how to present a case that gets her kids back with her. I have two more sessions to figure out how to do this."

I thought about how awful I felt because I'd given Brook the wrong telephone number. Compared with Rita's day, what I did seemed totally trivial. "How do you deal with things like that?" I said. "It would break my heart."

"I'm learning not to let it break mine. But it's hard. Really hard."

We looked at each other in silence for a while. Stella, the rabbit, started to snore. I looked at the time. It was midnight. "Time for me to hit the hay," I said.

Rita covered her mouth and yawned. "Big day tomorrow, girl."

"That's right." I stood up slowly. Tomorrow I would really pay a price for my manic running. "Thanks for the chat," I said.

"And thanks for the prosecco. We should do this again soon."

"Absolutely."

We hugged. It was like I was embracing a tiny bird.

The price of ambition

"I'd like you to sit in on this one," Richard had said that morning. He was the creative director for the Escalate account. "We're working on a campaign aimed at women and as you may have noticed, Tom and Frankie are both men."

Tom, the writer, sucked in his lips and primped an imaginary hairdo. Frankie, the designer, crossed his legs and wiggled.

"We always struggle to get the tone right for women," Richard said. "We need to inspire women but not talk to them like they're professional athletes. It's trickier than it seems. We could do with some of your female energy."

Richard was a bit out of shape, gentle and laidback, which was weird for the creative director of a sportswear account. He wore his hair in a ponytail, which didn't help. You'd think he would have been extra dynamic and athletic, like Jim the strategic director. Still, Richard was a sweet guy, devoted to his family. Ever since I'd been assigned to the Escalate account he'd gone out of his way to be nice and complimentary to me. I liked him.

At that moment in time, several hours later, I was focusing my female energy on writing down the rough concepts Tom and Frankie had worked up during the day. I also had the original brief in front of me to make sure that, in their excitement, they didn't lose sight of what they were supposed to be doing. When creatives got going they fired off ideas at an incredibly rapid rate and a concept could change into something completely different in minutes, which led to the danger of the work failing to meet the brief.

I loved watching the creatives going head to head and fighting for their ideas while Richard listened. Tom had just suggested building the campaign around promoting women's mass night runs. He'd called it "Taking back the night."

"That could work," Richard said. He glanced down at his watch. "Guys, I have to go now. My turn to make the school run. Sorry. But I think this is good work. It has potential. Push it some more and let me see something tomorrow morning. Don't forget, we've only got a day to get this right."

A look passed between Tom and Frankie. "Sure," Frankie said. "We'll have something for you first thing."

"Great. But don't work too late, guys. It might be better to leave the work to sit for a while and tackle it with fresh minds tomorrow. You've got time. Up to you." Richard's phone beeped. He had a message. He saw who it was from, threw on his jacket and was out the door in seconds.

"Fresh minds," Tom said. "What is that? Asshole. We've been working on this for a week now."

"And the weekend, don't forget" Frankie added. "He's supposed to give us creative direction, be our glorious leader, not disappear every time his wife clicks her fingers."

"How many kids does he have?" I asked.

"I dunno," Tom said. "Five, ten. What's that got to do with anything?"

I shrugged. I could see Tom's point.

"Anyway," Frankie said. "He doesn't know the first thing about design so his advice always sucks. We're better off without him."

"Maybe," Tom said, "but he gets paid way more than us to not give us advice. And it's not as if he adds anything to the writing. Dude's old school. Strictly eighties all the way."

"Whatever," Frankie said. "So, Lemon, you sticking around?"

"Sure," I said. "Um, can I ask you something? Why have you guys started calling me Lemon?"

"It actually refers to a momentous event in advertising history," Frankie said, adopting a deep TV announcer voice. "In 1959, the ad agency Doyle Dane Bernbach was given the challenge of advertising the Volkswagen, then the…" He looked at my earnest face and cracked up laughing. "No, Richard started calling you that."

"After Liz Lemon on 30 Rock?"

"Right."

"Cool. I like it."

———•———

I stayed at work with the creatives until they were happy with the new direction the campaign was taking. By the time we finished it was getting light. I'd never stayed that late before. But I was on a high. We'd taken a break to have dinner in the restaurant near The Agency that everyone went to, which they said they could claim back on expenses, but apart from that they worked solidly.

About eleven, I got a text from Rita telling me she'd made extra curry—she was an amazing cook—and did I want some. It made me feel kind of grown up to write back "I'd love to but I'm working late. Save me some, please."

"Good work, Lemon," Tom said over his shoulder as he placed the finished visuals for the campaign on Richard's desk. His voice was croaky with exhaustion.

"Yeah, thanks," added Frankie. "We couldn't have done it without you."

"What did I do?"

"I don't know," Tom said, "but, whatever you did, it was the essential missing ingredient."

"Thanks guys," I said. "See you in…" I looked at the time on my phone. "Oh my god, four hours."

"Actually, you won't see us," Frankie said. "We'll be sleeping in. We've done our bit. It's up to Richard to sell the work to account direction now."

"Oh," I said. "Maybe I won't go home then. I'll just have to turn around and come straight back."

"Cool," Tom said. "If you're going to stick around, why don't you present the concepts to Richard? We'll feel better."

"Right on," Frankie said.

"Cool," I said. Exhausted as I was, their faith in me gave me a huge lift.

Luckily, I always kept a spare set of gym clothes at work in case I found time to run in the morning. I hadn't found time yet so these were clean. I took a cold shower and slipped on the fresh t-shirt. It was Escalate so that was good. After I'd showered I took a good look at my face in the mirror. My eyes looked like a hundred miles of bad road.

I thought about what my mom had said about being punished for having ambition. I almost knew what she meant.

"How you doing, Lemon?" I said to myself in the mirror. "Pretty good," I told myself.

Pretty good.

Watching Richard go through the work Tom and Frankie had done gave me a good idea why he was the creative director and they weren't. I watched as he tweaked headlines until they really sang and gave detailed instructions as to how the design needed to change. At around mid-day, when Tom and Frankie still hadn't arrived, he gave the visuals to a designer in studio to work up for presentation to the accounts team.

"I have to go, Lemon, I'm afraid." Richard's voice startled me out of my trance. My gaze was fixed on my computer screen but my mind was completely elsewhere.

"Oh, okay," I said.

"Yeah, I've got to take one of the kids to the orthodontist. Kids. Who'd have them, ay?"

"No problem," I said. My voice sounded like it was coming from underwater.

"Could you show Tom and Frankie the visuals when they come back from the design studio, Lemon, please? If they don't make it in today, take the visuals to the accounts team yourself. That way I'll know they got there."

"Sure."

"And, Lemon. Don't take this the wrong way but please go home at a sensible time tonight."

"I love being here at night," I said. "It's when I feel The Agency really come alive."

"Maybe it does," Richard said. "I probably felt the same when I was your age. Listen, it's great that you're so dedicated. Believe it or not, I used to be like you and the guys. It was only when I stopped pulling all-nighters that I realized they were pretty much a waste of time. Your best ideas always come to you when you're fresh and relaxed, not when you've been staring at a screen or piece of paper for hours. I've lost count of the number of times I've woken up with the perfect line going round and round in my head at three in the morning, or when I've been in the shower. You can't force real creativity, Lemon. Remember that."

"I'll try, Richard," I said. "Thanks."

"Good. See you tomorrow."

———◆———

Next morning Richard was called in to see the Executive Creative Director, who had just been appointed. When he'd left, Tom looked at Frankie and smiled.

Richard was in shock when he came back. After he'd sat at his desk with his head in his hands for ten minutes he took a deep breath and came over to me.

"I've been let go, Liz," he said. "I didn't see it coming."

"Oh no," I said. I have to say that the first thing I thought was "What about me? What am I going to do now?" I felt horribly ashamed. "Do you know why?"

"I don't, Lemon. Maybe I'm just the wrong kind of guy for a sportswear account. It could be because I don't work around the clock like everyone else does. Who knows? Perhaps the client complained. But that new ECD's a hard bi...sorry," Richard said. "It wasn't enough to fire me. She had to go through every screw-up I've made since I've been here. There were a lot of them, apparently." He laughed. It was painful to hear. "When she finished, she just pointed to the door and said, "Why don't you just leave now?" so that's what I'm doing. I just wanted to ask you if you could take my laptop back to IT for me and clean out my desk for me. I just can't do it right now. I'll come back for my stuff later in the week."

"Sure," I said. "I'm so, so sorry." To be honest, my first thought was that Richard had been kicked out because he wasn't hungry enough. He was too nice for The Agency. And he had a life outside of this place.

"That's advertising for you, Lemon. Still, at least they stab you in the front here." He looked over at where Tom and Frankie were staring at their computers or pretending to. "Or at least I think they do. Anyway, I'm out of here. See you around, maybe. And good luck. Look after yourself. You'll be fine, I know it."

My eyes filled with tears. He looked like he was about to cry too. He stood up, walked back to his desk, picked up a photograph of his wife and children, and walked out the door without saying goodbye to anyone else and without looking back.

It felt like my future at The Agency had just walked out the door with him. Once I'd boxed up all of Richard's things I had no idea what to do next. I went from desk to desk asking people if there was anything I could do for them. Around the middle of the afternoon, I found a project to work on with the account's strategic planners. I was safe but I had no idea for how long.

I thought of the way Tom had smiled at Frankie. Had they known what was going to happen to Richard?

A revelation in the cave

A couple of days after Richard left, the Executive Creative Director who'd fired him called me into her office, which was actually in a space called the Cave. She said it was just to have a coffee but my heart sank. I'd been scrambling around to find things to do but I knew I wasn't really adding value to the team. Without anyone to assist, it made sense to let me go too.

Paradoxically or intentionally, the Cave was on the top floor of the building. To keep out the sunlight it was roofed with curved, ridged fabric which was meant to look like rocks veined with minerals. It was a space that was, in theory, set aside for relaxing and meditation. One of the founders of The Agency was heavily into yoga and meditation and firmly believed they helped enhance creativity. I'd been shown the Cave on my first tour of The Agency, I couldn't decide if it was cool or ridiculous.

The Cave had a wall of backlit, glowing rose quartz crystals. In one corner, water somehow ran up inside a tower of pebbles and trickled down over them in constant flow. Cushions in the shape of flat, round pebbles were scattered around the room for people to sit or lie on. Perhaps to take a little of the seriousness out of the whole thing, some of the cushions had spots of what was meant to look like bird poop on them.

Creatives who came to the Cave to find inspiration or take a nap had a shelf of new age music CDs to choose from and a library of self-help and spiritual books to read.

When I walked into the Cave I was surprised to see that the new ECD was a girl I'd first met as part of Brook's entourage. I hadn't seen her around much since then and perhaps her new role was the reason. I'd always felt she didn't like me much so my spirits dropped even further.

"How are you doing, Liz?" she said. "Pull up a pebble."

I lowered myself onto one of the cushions and perched on it with my coffee.

"Good."

She smiled, leaned forward. "Keeping busy?"

"I am." I took a deep breath. "I'm helping out with strategy for Escalate," I said.

"How is that working out?"

"Great," I tried not to sound overly sincere. "I love it."

"You were reporting directly to Richard, right?"

"I was."

"Doesn't him going leave you a bit short of things to do?"

I thought I saw where she was going with this. "Um..."

She smiled, a real, warm smile. "I'm sure it does, Liz." She looked around her. "Oh shoot, you must have thought...I'm so sorry. I just asked you to meet me in the Cave because it's nice and quiet. Don't worry, I'm not trying to get rid of you. I've asked around and everyone says they love having you on the team. We just need to find a better use of your talents."

"Really?" I was so relieved I squeaked. The ECD was polite enough not to laugh although I saw her mouth twitch as she suppressed a smile.

"Of course, Liz. So, listen, we'll be appointing a new creative director to the Escalate account very soon and I'd like you to figure out a way to work with that person. In the meantime, use your initiative. Make yourself useful, work with Tom and Frankie, and hang in there."

"Will do. Thank you so much."

"You don't need to thank me, Liz. People obviously think you've got a lot to offer The Agency. I'm not going to argue with them." Her laptop beeped. "Right. That's my next meeting." The ECD stood up, gave me her hand to shake. I realized I hadn't touched my coffee.

As I walked out of the Cave door, which had been open throughout our meeting, the ECD called out "Keep up the good work, Liz." It sounded just a little bit too theatrical.

Walking back to my floor, I tried to process how nice the ECD had been to me after the way she'd treated Richard. I couldn't. I thought about what she'd said about working with Tom and Frankie. I was sure one or both of them had something to do with Richard being let go. I would watch them from now on, making sure I didn't get too close.

I sat down at my desk, tapped my mouse to bring my computer screen to life, and a vision of Richard being fired while sitting on a giant bird shit-covered pebble popped into my head.

———•———

While I figured out what I was going to do next, I kept my head down. Although I struggled to fill my days, I still stayed late. This was partly because, despite my growing friendship with Rita, I still didn't have much of a life. But it was also because hanging out at The Agency after hours helped me broaden my understanding of how the place worked. I ended up doing a couple of voice-overs for Escalate, was an extra in a commercial for a cancer charity, and my hands were used in a photoshoot.

———•———

I was sitting at my computer one evening switching between Facebook and a report I was working on for Escalate basketball, when a girl I'd never seen before sat down on the corner of my desk. "You're Liz, right?" she said. "I'm Kat."

I looked up from my screen and waited for my eyes to refocus so I could see her properly. The first thing I noticed was her glasses. They made her look like Thelma from Scooby Doo. "Hi, Kat. Pleased to meet you."

"Brook told me to find you. I've got this idea and she thought you'd be the perfect person to help me with it."

"Tell me more," I said.

"Shall we go get a beer somewhere?"

"Sure."

———•———

"So that's it," Kat said. "What do you think?"

"Wow. It's a great idea. I'd love to be involved."

"That's why I'm talking to you," Kat said. "I saw that research report you put together for the Escalate Olympics campaign. It was impressive, and really creative, Lemon." She must have seen the startled look on my face because she said "They do call you Lemon, don't they? That's what Tom called you when I told him I was looking for you."

"They do call me Lemon, yes."

"Cool nickname. I wish I had a nickname. You know that Lemon comes from that brilliant DDB ad campaign for Volkswagen, right?"

"I do, yeah. But they told me it comes from Liz Lemon. You know, on 30 Rock."

Kat laughed. "Oh, yeah. Perfect."

I felt so proud that I had a nickname. Perhaps I really belonged at The Agency.

———•———

Kat and I started to meet at least once a week to plan how we would present our proposal to the strategy department. I realized she was seriously ambitious and efficient. It didn't take me long to see that working with her could really take me places inside The Agency.

After a couple of months of planning, we pitched our two-girl research team idea to the strategic directors on all of The Agency's accounts. It was obviously what they'd been waiting for. Our days and a large portion of our nights were soon spent doing online research, creating surveys and journals for people to complete, and devising enticing ways for them to try out products made by The Agency's clients. My favorite part of what we did was interviewing and filming people for our clients— talking to athletes for Escalate in particular.

I'd known I loved research from my Denver days. Now I was infatuated. But I was beginning to realize the truth of what my mom had said about the price of ambition.

One night I got home about midnight, an early night for me. I grabbed a bottle of Prosecco from the fridge and a glass, put them on a tray with a couple of slices of pizza I'd taken from The Agency, freshly microwaved, and headed for my room. There was no sound coming from Rita's room so I had no one to wind down with. I was so fired up from work that I couldn't sleep. I drank all of the Prosecco and I was so hungry that I ate all of the pizza as well as most of a tub of ice-cream. Once again, I made a vow to get up extra-early and go running the next morning.

I was still wide awake at 3 am when I finally climbed into bed to try and sleep. I couldn't understand how I could be exhausted and still buzzing with energy. Ideas for how Kat and I could improve what we offered whirled around my head but my stomach was horribly bloated and painful. I could hear the sounds of The Agency in my head—the clashing music, the conversations, shouts of laughter. I'd had this feeling before but never so bad.

At least I had two weeks of Christmas vacation coming up.

———◆———

By the time I knew when I could take time off for my vacation—a week—tickets home were crazy expensive. I flew on Christmas Day with stopovers in Phoenix and Vegas. I saw a guy I used to go to high school with in the airport at Vegas but his liberal use of eyeliner took me by surprise and I didn't have a chance to say "Hi."

I wondered how much I'd changed since school. I certainly felt a lot more grown up and sophisticated than the guy with makeup.

Back at home I slept most of the time and snuggled back into my pre-adult, pre-The Agency life. My mom made a few comments about how tired I looked. But, thanks to a regime of running, eating properly and early nights, I started to feel pretty good. Life in Saint Paul was slow, relaxed, and most of all, familiar.

But that familiarity was also a problem. I didn't want to revert to being a child who is called for dinner, with my Mom washing my clothes, and having to ask to borrow the car. I wanted to make something of myself and the best chance I had to do that was in Seattle with The Agency.

One night I was out with a gang of friends from high school and college. They were mostly supportive of me and what I was doing. After we'd had a few drinks, one guy looked me in the eye and said "But, Liz, you're toooo nice for advertising."

"I'm not," I said. "Not that you would know. How's it working out for you at Staples?"

Enter Chloe

I came back to work after Christmas, refreshed and determined to change the way I worked. That lasted for three days. I just couldn't find a way to leave The Agency at what would have been a reasonable time every night. Sometimes I got halfway to the door but I always turned around and went back. You could say I was addicted but it just felt weird, and somehow disloyal, to leave when everyone else was working. The feeling of us all being in it together was also fun. I didn't want to miss out on anything.

One of the things I loved was the pranks that people played on each other. When you put a bunch of highly creative, fired up, mostly young people together it's going to happen. My favorite was when a creative director who everyone really liked had his entire work space moved two floors down from where it usually was. As soon as he'd left for the night, his whole team mobilized. They took photos of where everything was on his desk and bookshelves and put them back in exactly the same place. It must have taken hours of meticulous effort. Far from being annoyed, the creative director loved the prank and didn't move his desk back for a couple of days.

I hoped for and dreaded the time when I would be worthy of having a prank played on me.

For now, I became more and more of a trusted face at The Agency and people began to let their hair and their guard down around me. I may have started out as Liz "too nice for advertising" but more and more people were calling me Lemon, which I loved.

Having a nickname made me feel like I belonged, as if I was in a band. Of course, The Agency encouraged us to think of what we were doing as rock and roll. This was rock and roll in the Rolling Stones "excess in all areas but always do a great show and take care of business" sense. "Live fast and if you don't die young, make some dough and retire." Encouraging us to think of ourselves as rockers was a smart move. It gave us the kind of swagger and sense that we were the best in the game that all good musicians have. We were in it together. A band of rebel artists following our own rules.

But, if thinking of ourselves as advertising's answer to rock gods was good for The Agency, it wasn't always so great for the guys and girls in the band.

———◆———

I got used to seeing people at parties disappear into the bathroom and come out sniffing, glassy-eyed and talking incredibly fast, usually about themselves. What shocked me was realizing why they all looked so much fresher than me the morning after, even if the party hadn't wound down until the early hours.

One morning I was in the bathroom, splashing water on my face, pinching my cheeks and trying to look perky. From one of the cubicles came a loud sniff that echoed around the bathroom. I giggled and the girl inside the cubicle said "Whoops."

Silence, followed by another loud sniff.

"Wanna bump?" the voice said.

"No thanks." My voice sounded horribly Midwestern and ultra-polite and I made a face at myself in the mirror.

"Don't mind if I don't, eh?" the voice said. The lavatory flushed, the door was unlocked and Chloe exploded into my life.

"So you don't indulge?" Chloe said, as she checked under her nose for any tell-tale signs.

"Um…" I said.

"Don't know why I'm even bothering to do this." She rubbed her nose one last time before applying a coat of the brightest pink red lipstick I'd ever seen. "No one here gives a shit, anyway. So, like I say, you don't indulge?"

"I like Adderall," I said. "I wouldn't mind some of that."

"Not a problem," Chloe said. "You can get anything you want here, girl. It's what they call an open secret."

"Anything?"

"Okay, not the really hard stuff. Smack, crack, meth. But anything else, sure." She reeled off a long list of drugs I'd never heard of. I didn't dare ask what they actually did.

By the time Chloe finished, I felt like the most innocent little girl to have ever skipped out of the Midwest. She was to become my guide into the secret underworld of The Agency and, for a time, my best friend.

———◆———

Chloe had been a commercial producer. According to Brook she was one of the best The Agency ever had. She could party all night and still be on set at four in the morning. Someone who worked with her once told me that seeing tiny Chloe, who liked to wear big boots and a leather jacket, telling a crew of 150 enormous tattooed teamsters what to do was a master class in the art of production. When it came to keeping a Hollywood star or athlete happy, Chloe was the queen of schmoozing. They didn't impress her much so if the kid gloves approach failed she didn't hesitate to resort to threats so subtle someone else would probably never have known they were being made.

Most of all, Chloe's loyalty was to The Agency and, for as long as they were shooting together, the director.

It was her boyfriend who had made Chloe's glittering career as a producer. If it hadn't been for him, she'd have graduated to Hollywood herself. He was a skinny, long-haired musician, from somewhere back East like she was. Like many musicians, it seemed, he hadn't quite come to grips with the concepts of hard work or fidelity. Chloe gave up on commercial production because she was tormented by what went through her head when she was away on commercial shoots.

"I was also getting too old," Chloe told me. "I'm thirty-four and that's dangerously close to being put out to pasture. Being great at what you do is only half the game. You've also got to be as cute as you are hungry. And there's always someone snapping at your heels. I got tired of looking over my shoulder at the next lipstick shark heading for my ass. So now I work in digital production. It's as boring as a Coldplay song but, you know, it'll do until I figure out what I want to do next."

Chloe's boyfriend, we'll call him Cody, told her he needed his own space to create so they didn't live together. Whenever we were out together she would end up calling him, her voice turning into that of a little, insecure girl, and unless he brushed her off she'd trot off to his apartment.

As I got to know Chloe better I realized that what she really wanted was to be with Cody, have his babies, and give it all up. Or, that was half of what she wanted. Like me, she was addicted to The Agency—probably more than the coke she couldn't stop snorting.

Chloe scared me but she was so much fun.

———•———

Apart from me, and I have no idea why she liked me so much, Chloe's friends were all in their thirties and forties. They were still capable of being wild but, like one woman who worked in the legal department and had a boyfriend in a semi big name band, they were trying to settle down and turn what they loved into a career.

Kat, my partner in our two-person research team, was just thirty. Setting up the research team was partly her way of making her mark at The Agency and looking to the future. "I'm on track," was how she put it to me.

I didn't ask Kat to spell out what she meant. I figured that she, a Midwesterner like me but one who'd travelled and acquired a veneer of international sophistication, had strayed quite a ways off track in her time.

The Agency also hired people who had been famous themselves. In my time, a girl who'd been the singer and main songwriter in a punky riot girl band worked as an assistant to the creative director on the Escalate account, my old job, although not for long. Working at The Agency was a bit too much off track for her.

One time Kat and I were walking past a glass-sided conference room on my floor on our way to a meeting when I noticed a girl sitting, obviously waiting to be interviewed for a job. She had the same expression I must have worn all those months ago. I did a double-take because she looked incredibly familiar.

"Is that who I think it is?" I said to Kat.

"Looks like it," Kat said. She pretended to be nonchalant but I knew she was as amazed as I was.

The girl in the glass-sided room had been at the center of a presidential scandal when she was an intern at the White House.

Odin's Beard

Pretty soon Chloe started arriving at my desk around 11 every night and we'd always end up having at least one big glass of wine. Chloe was on a mission to have the best night ever, every single night, and I often left her as she was heading off to some late-night dive. I, however, was determined not to blow the opportunity Kat had presented me with so I was careful to stop at one glass—or at least try to do so.

I admired the way Kat could party just enough without going over the edge and I was trying to follow her example.

One Thursday night Chloe and I were sitting at my desk munching pizza left by someone who'd been working on a pitch. By this time, we'd normally be planning our weekend's partying. On weekends, shy retiring Liz Lemon let her hair down, pulled on her motorcycle boots, and all bets were off, especially if Cody, Chloe's on-off boyfriend, wasn't around. Or, worse, if he'd suggested they break up.

Chloe was an excellent mimic. The impression she did of Cody saying "Uh, maybe we should break up," as if he was stoned and was suggesting they go out for burritos, was hilarious. They'd been together for eight years. Or as together as Cody could ever be.

"Why don't we go to a Bikram yoga class tomorrow night?" Chloe said, taking an enormous bite of pizza.

"A what?"

"It's some kind of hot yoga class. All the cool people are doing it."

"I'm not cool."

"True. But I am."

"Hah! True. But why should we go to a hot yoga class when we could be partying?"

"We can party any time. And we already know what the parties are going to be like, who's going to be there, what they're going to say. All that stuff. You'll stand in the corner waiting for Mr Right-Now to talk to you and he never will. And I'll get so bored I'll take some horrific drug that makes me think I'm a giant fish. It'll just be the same ol' same ol.' Next morning we'll ask ourselves why we do this shit." Chloe put on her deep, smooth TV announcer voice. "So why not change your life this weekend and try Bikram yoga? It's the hottest thing going."

Going back to her normal voice, Chloe said, "Seriously, Liz. I think I'm partying too much. I want to get healthy before I forget what it was like. And, who knows, we might meet a couple of hot, hot, hot yoga guys. Come on, girl. It'll be fun. Well, it probably won't but you know what I mean."

I thought about it. Partying with Chloe was awesome but getting into Bikram might be a way to tone it down a little. I could do without waking up every single Monday morning feeling like I'd done a toxic triathlon. "Okay. But you owe me."

And so it was that we found ourselves sitting on yoga mats on a Friday night when we would normally have been perched on bar stools. I had some halfway decent yoga gear, although I felt overdressed compared to the nearly naked ultra-lean yogis who surrounded us. Chloe wore a faded Black Flag t-shirt and leggings. I knew she'd made a terrible mistake but I hoped I might get out alive. We were both already sweating.

Back in 2006 Bikram yoga was literally the hottest form of yoga around. It still is, actually. The formula was and is simple. You practice a basic sequence of twenty-six yoga poses in a room heated to between 95 and 108 degrees Fahrenheit with a humidity factor of forty degrees. The sheer severity of Bikram made it a big draw for people who wanted to push themselves but also to be seen as seriously hardcore.

One wall of the yoga studio was given over to a mirror so we yogis could watch ourselves practicing the postures. This, of course, meant that a lot of sneaky peeking (at abs, biceps, glutes and whatever) went on. Our own and other people's.

I'd done yoga off and on since college in Denver and, despite the excesses of life at The Agency, I thought of myself as fit. Sitting cross-legged on my mat, I was excited to the point of being slightly fearful about what was going to happen. Chloe had gone very quiet. The veteran Bikram yogis were eyeing us overdressed newbies with snotty, superior expressions.

We started off slow but, even so, ten minutes into the 90-minute class, Chloe went from bright red to deathly white and staggered to the door. Maybe I should have gone after her but there was no way I was going to quit. By that time, I'd figured out that this wasn't the laidback yoga I was used to. The people I was practising with were deadly serious. Which brought out my competitive spirit.

Although I came close that first session, I didn't give up. By the time we finished and were lying down in Savasana, the relaxation posture, I was more relaxed than I'd ever been in my life. When the teacher knelt beside me and sprayed my aching feet with an essential oil spray I was in ecstasy.

Getting dressed after the class I felt a real camaraderie with my fellow Bikram yogis. It was as if we'd survived a little battle together. And when I caught sight of myself in the mirror it looked like I'd already lost a few pounds. I curled my left arm and patted my hard bicep. I felt like Mrs Thor. "Odin's beard," I whispered.

A tall guy with an armful of tattoos nodded at me and said "First time?"

"Yep," I said.

He nodded again and went back to getting dressed. I had no idea whether he approved of me or not. Luckily my face was still bright red so no one could see I was blushing.

It was only when I was walking out of the yoga studio into the cold, rainy Seattle night that I realized I'd completely forgotten about Chloe. When I checked my cell phone I saw a message from her telling me to meet her in a bar nearby. It ended with "You'll never guess who's here."

———•———

I prayed that Chloe's message didn't mean she'd found some terrifying new drug she was determined to try. But when I spotted her in the bar, she had some colour in her cheeks. And she was sitting with Sean, the enigmatic older creative I'd been wondering about since he first started manufacturing reasons to bump into me. They were both sniffing so I had a good idea what they'd been doing. I wondered if he'd called Chloe and asked if she was out with me. I didn't mind.

I walked over to them as gracefully as I could. My legs were still trembling from the hot yoga.

"Look who I bumped into," Chloe said. "I was just telling Sean about our near-death experience."

"Yours," I said, allowing Sean to give me a peck on the cheek. "I did all right. I'm going back next week."

I liked the way Sean was looking at me, as if I was the last glass of water in the desert.

"Ayee," Chloe said. "Don't want to lose my buddy Lemon to hot yoga Nazis. What are you having? We're celebrating being alive."

"Do we need an excuse?" Sean asked.

"Guess not," Chloe said, waving an arm to attract a waiter. She turned to me, smiled and stage-whispered "That bastard Cody has broken up with me again."

"Don't worry," I said.

"Nah. It's different this time. I've had enough." The waiter arrived. Chloe looked him up and down. "Tequila. Nine shots, amigo. And make it snappy. Three Tecates too."

Sean looked at me and winked. I shrugged. I'd survived hot yoga. I was Mrs. Thor. A few tequilas weren't going to kill me. When the first round arrived, I led the charge and threw mine back. "Odin's Beard," I shouted as it went down.

"Odin's Beard," Sean boomed, downing his shot and gulping Tecate.

"Odin's Beard indeed," Chloe said. She did her three tequilas in one go and drained half her Tecate. "Here's to the single life." She swivelled on her barstool to look up at me "Odin's Beard?"

"It's what Thor says in the comics," Sean said. "Right, Lemon?"

"It is," I said. "Here we go," I thought.

"I bought you this, Liz." The voice was Sean's. My eyes snapped open. At first I thought I was at home in my own bed. Mercifully I'd just crashed out on one of the bar's overstuffed retro couches. Sean stood in front of me with a small bottle of water.

I sat up, winced as my stomach muscles protested and drank half the water in one mouthful. "Thanks. How long have I been asleep?"

"About an hour. We were all dancing and in a split second you were out on your feet. I got you over here and you fell fast asleep."

"My hero."

"Odin's Beard." Sean leaned forward and kissed me lightly on the lips. "Shall we get you home?"

"You stay," I said. I looked over to where Chloe was whirling madly on the dance floor. "Chloe needs you to keep her safe, I think. So do I. And I really do need to get up and out of this sofa while I can still move."

Sean held out his hands. I took them in mine and he pulled me up. He was surprisingly strong. We hugged and held hands as we went to tell Chloe I was leaving. Something flashed across her face as she saw us. Looking at her eyes and twitching mouth I figured she'd continued making regular trips to the bathroom.

The taxi Sean called for me was waiting outside. It was raining and he took off his jacket and held it over my head as he walked me to the car. He turned my face up to his, kissed me a little longer and harder this time.

He pulled away. "Odin's Beard," he said, shaking his head. "Call you in the morning, Lemon. Get some sleep."

Oh My G.O.S.H.

Despite the Tequila-Tecate hangover and a body that ached so much it felt like someone had banged nails into my thighs, I woke up on Saturday morning with a huge smile on my face. The last piece of the puzzle of my life in Seattle had fallen into place. I now had a great job, amazing social life, cool apartment, and a boyfriend!

I took a long hot shower and took my time getting dressed. I kept checking my cellphone but there was nothing from Sean. But if he'd carried on partying with Chloe that would make sense. I wasn't too worried.

There was no answer from Rita when I tapped on her door to see if she wanted to go for coffee at the bistro around the corner from the apartment. I went by myself. The guy who served me my coffee gave me a big smile. I was obviously radiating something. The rain had stopped and there wasn't a cloud in the sky so I took my coffee outside, put on my shades and tried not to check my phone every thirty seconds.

Around twelve, when Sean still hadn't called, I went back to my apartment. I knocked on Rita's door again. Nothing. At two I called Chloe.

"I'm just heading out the door," she said. "I'll call you when I get home." Her voice was a croaking monotone.

"Where are you at? Cody's? You guys made up?"

"No, Lemon. I'm just leaving Sean's. Total dump. I thought art directors were supposed to be tidy."

It felt like she'd punched me in the gut. I knew I didn't need to ask the next question but I did anyway.

There was a pause and then Chloe said "Are you serious, Lemon. Haven't you heard of the Oh My G.O.S.H group?"

"Yeah, but I don't know what it means."

"Lemon. It means Oh My Got On Sean Higgins."

"Oh."

"You've experienced him in action now, Lemon."

"Stop calling me Lemon."

"Sorry. Look, we all know Sean is handsome, charming, and a miracle cure for any relationship heartbreak or loneliness that ails a gal. It starts with that deep, soulful stare. Right?"

When I didn't say anything, Chloe carried on. "It's a bit corny but it works. I am so totally over Cody." Finally, my silence registered with Chloe. "Lemon…"

"I told you, don't call me Lemon."

"Sorry. Did you want to date him or something?" I said nothing. "Oh My God!" she screamed. "You totally did! Liz, what were you thinking of? The guy is beautiful, for sure, but as dumb as a doornail, and boring. I saved you from making a terrible mistake."

Chloe carried on talking about how she had no idea what made me think I was going to get something going with Sean. She said she'd steer me in the right direction and find the right guy for me.

Chloe was speaking so fast that I couldn't get a word in edgewise to make her admit that she'd done a pretty shitty thing. I'd seen her eyes narrow when Sean and I found her on the dance-floor. But I was as ashamed as I was mad. I felt like a complete fool. Screaming at Chloe would have made me look even more stupid and she knew it.

Finally I said "I'm in line to get a burrito. Got to go." And I cut Chloe off before she could say anything. I knew that was the end of our friendship and that I was never going to fall for another of Sean's soulful stares.

———◆———

I finally fell asleep around 6 a.m. on Sunday morning and was awakened by a horrifically loud banging on the door. I went out into the hall. Rita was standing, looking at the door, wearing a man's t-shirt, her arms wrapped around herself. "That's Sam's boyfriend," she said. "If he's out drinking late in the city, after the trams have stopped running, he stays over. I'm sure he'll go away."

The banging continued for another ten minutes and then stopped. Rita and I looked at each other and started to move towards our bedrooms. "Hope you don't mind me saying this, but you don't look so good. Let's catch up later. I'll cook for you."

"I'd like that," I said.

She stepped inside her bedroom and closed the door. I heard a male voice say something to which she answered, "My hero," before cackling with laughter.

I'd just climbed back into bed when the banging started again, this time at the back door. It carried on for another few minutes then stopped. Silence. Then banging at the front door. I'd had enough by now. I stomped down the hallway, yanked the front door open so hard it almost pulled the security chain out of the frame, and was confronted by the meekest looking specimen of a guy I'd ever seen.

"Yes?"

"Sam?" He was reeling drunk.

"Not here," I said, slamming the door. There was no more knocking.

I went back to bed and, after another hour of tossing and turning, fell into a deep, dreamless sleep that lasted until Sunday evening.

By then it all caught up with me. I felt like I'd gone fifteen rounds with Iron Mike Tyson. I crawled out to the store—it took me half an hour to walk two blocks—and picked up some Nyquil and Dayquil, Brook's magical elixir.

On Monday morning I washed the Dayquil down with coffee and crawled into the office. Although I felt awful, I also felt kind of grown-up. Was this what being an adult was really all about?

Without ever apologizing, Chloe tried to keep our friendship alive. The first couple of times she showed up after that horrible weekend, perched on my desk, and said, "Vino?" I told her I was too busy. After I did this twice more, she got the message and stopped coming around. I was kind of sad because Chloe was incredibly fun and somewhere inside was a good person. But she was dangerous. I didn't see Sean for a week or so, until he turned up in a meeting Kat and I called to present some research findings. I was dreading seeing him again but when I did the dangerous allure had gone. He looked small, tired, and old. I could feel his eyes on me when I was presenting, but what was once exciting now just felt creepy. He waited for me at the door to the meeting room and I thoroughly enjoyed sweeping past him as I locked eyes with Kat and said, "What do you know about organic tampons?"

"I use them, actually."

I felt rather than saw Sean skulk off.

We turned a corner and Kat said, "What was all that about?"

"All what?"

"The bad vibes you were giving Sean in that meeting could have flattened a building." She stopped, looked me in the eye. "You didn't? Did you?"

"Join the Oh My G.O.S.H. club? Of course not."

We kept walking. As we were click-clacking down the stairs to our floor, Kat started to giggle. "I did," she said.

"You did what? Oh!"

I started to laugh, hard. When I tried to control my laughter a loud snort came out. Kat looked at me in surprise and burst into laughter. She dragged me into a bathroom and we laughed until she said "Oh my gosh, I'm going to pee my pants" and dashed into a stall.

That set us off again. I kept laughing from outside the stall. I don't have any control over the sounds that come out of my nose when I laugh but I have complete bladder control.

———◆———

Now that my friendship with Chloe was over and Sean was out of the picture, it was probably inevitable that I'd drift back into Brook's orbit. I'd missed her, found her inspiring. She made me feel safe. Even if I didn't exactly know where I was headed, I told myself that being part of Brook and Company was as much of a smart move careerwise as it was a desire or even need to be Brook's friend. Brook had plenty to teach me about the advertising industry and, I hoped, about life.

Brook, unfortunately, thought I was adorable. She once told me she could imagine me baking muffins every Saturday and handing them out to my neighbors. I think she meant it as a compliment. But having someone you hero-worship say that they always picture you baking is not exactly flattering. Still, now that I'd walked on the wild side a little with Chloe, I knew that wholesome, "too nice for advertising" Liz was only part of who I was. As was Liz Lemon. I just hadn't found the rest of me yet.

I also wanted to get to know the girls in Brook's entourage better, and not just because they were really fun. Although they were always perfectly dressed and looked like they didn't try too hard, they were also tough. They had to survive in an industry that was still dominated by men. Most of them were commercial producers. They couldn't afford to mess up because there was always another, younger, girl ready to step into their shoes and work twice as hard for half the money.

Being a part of Brook and Company was probably my best chance to meet a guy who wasn't a total loser.

———◆———

One Thursday I was deeply engrossed in some research when an email from Brook popped into my inbox. The email exchange went like this:

"Any plans for Friday?"

"Nope."

"Wanna come out with me and the girls Friday night? Birthday celebration."

"Yours?"

"Nope. You don't know her."

"Awesome. I'm honored. Sure."

"Awesome indeed. Wear something cute. We'll swing by your desk at eight."

"Wow, thanks."

"Don't thank me. Yet."

I was thrilled. It didn't occur to me ask why Brook would invite me to the birthday party of a girl I didn't know and who had no idea who I was.

After crab cakes and champagne at the gang's favorite bar we headed off to a club with live music on the east side of the city. The birthday girl's present was concert tickets and bottle service. We dumped our jackets at the banquette that had been reserved for us and strutted downstairs. I almost felt cool. We pushed our way to the front of the stage and danced to the band, which was fronted by a skinny girl singer with a huge vintage guitar, a full sleeve of tattoos covering one arm and bright red hair.

It was the kind of place Chloe would have haunted with Cody but, unless she lurked in the shadows, I didn't see her.

I jumped up and down for a couple of songs, breathing deeply that fabulous rock and roll scent of leather, perfume, sweat, dry ice, and pot until it felt like my ears were bleeding. I was making my way through the crowd in search of a bit of quiet when I felt someone put their hands on my shoulders and begin pushing me from behind. I looked around, straight into the grinning, sweating, perfectly gorgeous face of Brook. I laughed and let her drive me through the crowd of hard, damp bodies like I was a soft battering ram. Everyone we pushed past just laughed.

When we were at the edge, Brook took me by the hand and led me to the upstairs bar. This was a nicely quiet, dark, and funky place with plenty of nooks and crannies in which to hide away. Brook led us past people making out and doing who knows what else in the shadows to an empty booth. She waved her hand and a waiter appeared out of nowhere.

"Name your poison, Liz," Brook said.

"Um, just water, please."

Brook narrowed her eyes. "Not wimping out on us are you Liz?"

"Pacing myself."

"Smart move, girl. Mind if I don't join you?"

"Not at all."

"Great. A water and I'll have a vodka soda with lemon." The waiter, instantly smitten with Brook, floated away into the red velvet.

"How do you do it?" I asked.

"Order a drink?" Brook said.

I laughed. "No, although I am in awe of your ability to materialize waiters out of nowhere. I could have sat here by myself for hours and nothing would have happened. I must have the most ignorable face in the world."

"You don't, Liz. Trust me." Brook patted my hand. "But there's something bothering you, right?" Brook was amazing. No one else had noticed and I had thought I was hiding it well but there was no hiding from Brook.

I poured out the whole story of Chloe and Sean. Brook was silent until I finished. "So," she said. "You really are one of The Agency elite now, Liz."

"What do you mean?"

"You managed not to join Oh MY G.O.S.H. Unlike…"

"You didn't?"

"Moi? Good God, no." Brook laughed. Somehow, through all that noise, the barman heard her, turned and smiled.

"But it's so hard finding a guy," I said. "I felt so happy when I woke up after kissing Sean. It was like, I've got my great job, my apartment and now—ta-dah!—I've got the guy. Boy, was I wrong. How did you find Josh?"

"I don't know," Brook said. "I guess it was more that he found me and didn't take 'no' for an answer. I didn't want an agency romance, believe me. So, you're worried you're going to stay single forever, right? And you can't understand it, what with you being so cute and all. Never having had trouble finding a boy before."

"Kinda."

"Well, baby, if you look closely there's real romance all around you at work. Not just people hooking up out of loneliness, desperation or because they're in a chemically altered state. People find each other all the time. They just don't talk about it. The difference between Josh and me and everyone else was that we just didn't feel like we had anything to hide. Also, we're lucky. We're pretty high up on the totem pole and, as long as we stay discreet, no one's going to give us a hard time. Which all sounds great, I know. But I have to tell you I still don't have much of a personal life. Josh and I don't get to curl up on the sofa in front of a movie or walk the dogs on the beach all that often."

"You have dogs?"

"It was a figure of speech, sweetheart."

"But even if I do find a guy who isn't 'Mr. Right-now' or an asshole, what about all the other stuff? Babies, starting a family. How do I do this and have kids. I thought about freezing my eggs."

"Liz! You're only twenty-three."

"Twenty-four actually."

"When was your birthday?"

"Last month. I wanted to keep it quiet." I didn't have the heart to tell Brook that Chloe and I had gone on an almighty two-girl bender to celebrate my birthday.

"No worries. We can celebrate tonight. But, freezing your eggs? It's a bit drastic, isn't it?"

"I could wait until I'm thirty."

"It's also crazy expensive."

"It's not that unusual. Plenty of women are doing it," I said.

"Some of the big companies are already offering to freeze their female employees' eggs for free. So they can achieve their full potential or whatever. You think The Agency would do that?"

"I really don't know. But how do you feel about freezing your eggs?" I asked.

"I think it's kinda creepy, to be honest. One of those ideas that sounds good but if you stop and consider it for a while it's full of all kinds of dubious shit. At some point companies need to allow their employees time to date, have sex, and be present as parents. I don't think you've got anything to worry about Liz."

"What do you mean?"

"I've got the feeling you won't make it to thirty with us. I'm not criticizing you but I think you really are too nice for advertising. Or too sane. But, hey, I have no problem if you prove me wrong. And the other thing is…"

The waiter arrived with Brook's drink and my water. He placed the drinks on our table as if he was a geisha. All six foot four of him—tattooed, bearded and buff. Brook ordered a bottle of champagne and then waved him away as if he was a fly. But with consummate grace. I'm sure he thought he had a chance even as he floated back to the bar.

"What other thing, Brook? Tell me!"

"Have you seen the way Nate has been looking at you?"

"Who's Nate?"

We can be superheroes

It wasn't difficult to maneuver Nate into inviting me out on a date. I loved watching his delight when I said yes to the invitation I'd engineered and his attempts to mask this with cool.

I realized I'd seen him before at The Agency Halloween party. He was dressed as Superman. Although I'm more of a Batman girl, Nate made a nice Superman, and he filled out his costume nicely. I'd gone to the party dressed as Sif, the god Thor's wife.

As we took our first stumbling steps at conversation, I sneaked a proper look at Nate. He was six foot one with black hair and kind, bright blue eyes hidden behind the glasses he wore when he wasn't being Superman and a boy's open smile. If he had been from Iowa I would have sworn he was Clark Kent.

We made the date for a Wednesday. My thinking was that it wouldn't appear as big a deal as a weekend date. But, of course, I had butterflies in my stomach all day, as I hoped he did.

If you're surprised by the Sif reference, let me explain. I have a deep love of Norse mythology. It comes from being of Swedish origin and the idea that my ancestors were Vikings who had crossed the sea to America hundreds of years before Columbus. I grew up in Saint Paul, the capital of Minnesota, near the cities of New Sweden, Stockholm, and Uppsala. There were more Swedes in my part of the world than anywhere else in the Americas.

Norse mythology led to, or collided with, being a huge comic book fan. Which was one of the things that made me realize I perhaps wasn't quite like other girls.

I figured out early on that comic books say plenty about the world and the time in which they're written. For example, Captain America was created during WWII as a patriotic super-soldier who would inspire people to support the US's war effort. After America entered the war citizens were asked to make significant sacrifices. Captain America made them feel proud of what America was doing and why they were struggling. Comics and superheroes have also played a huge part in shaping the way I see the world.

I grew up around boys and every afternoon we'd watch X-Men or Batman on TV. The boys would choose which superhero they were and ask me who I was. My options were Storm who could control the weather, Jean Grey who is telepathic and can see the future or Batgirl, one of Batman's sidekicks. I would always be Storm even though, weirdly enough, controlling the weather didn't really seem that exciting. Really, I wanted to be Batman.

Batman wasn't born with special powers. He was extraordinary because he chose to be. And there wasn't a female character around back then like Batman. Mainstream comic book creators weren't interested in dreaming up female characters who were as strong as their male counterparts, which obviously said something about American society at the time.

The only case of female empowerment I can think of back in the eighties was Barbara Gordon, PhD, AKA Batgirl. After Batgirl was paralyzed from the waist down as a result of being shot by the Joker, in the 1988 graphic novel Killing Joke by the fantastic Alan Moore, she got into computers.

Also in 1988 a character by the name of Oracle appeared in Yale and Ostrander's Suicide Squad. Oracle was a brilliant hacker and badass who used her genius and skill with computers to fight crime. In 1990 Oracle was revealed to be Batgirl. To this day she remains the one superhero with a disability. I love the idea of being a hacker PhD crime fighter.

The best thing about comic books for me is the way they're nearly always a simple conflict between good and evil, light and dark. Thor's hammer would only ever strike the unjust before returning to his hand. In real life, the line between good and evil often seems blurred but perhaps it's always clear.

———◆———

"You're the only person I've met from Salt Lake City who isn't a Mormon," I said.

Nate smiled. "Weird, huh. I was actually born in New Orleans."

"Which explains quite a bit. Like the Harley and the leather jacket."

"I'm sure there are plenty of Mormons who ride a motorcycle."

"Bikers for Jesus."

"Joseph's Angels."

(I later found out that there was actually a motorcycle club called the Stormin' Mormons.)

"So how come New Orleans? And how come Salt Lake City?"

"Army brat," Nate said. "Family moved around a lot. I was always the new kid in town. And," he shrugged. "I was a fattie introvert, which didn't help."

"I knew you were a fattie!" I said and then clapped my hand

over my mouth. "Oh God," I said. "I didn't mean it like that."

Nate blushed and his eyes narrowed. "Um, why?" he said.

"Because you don't know how cute you are," I said. "Guys who've always been in shape kind of take it for granted and you can see it in how they carry themselves and how they act at the same time. You don't do this. That's nice."

Nate beamed. He gave up on any pretense of being cool. "Well, thank you lil lady," he said in the worst "aw shucks" N'awlins accent. "Another drink?"

"I have to say I prefer farm boys from the rolling cornfields of Iowa". Nate looked baffled. He hadn't picked up on my reference to Superman's origins. He obviously wasn't a comic book fan. I tried a different tactic, fluttering my eyelashes, "But I have always depended on the kindness of strangers."

Nate's eyes were locked on mine as he signaled to the waiter by raising his arm over his head. He looked blank. "Um, sorry?" He didn't get the Blanche Dubois, Streetcar Named Desire reference either. So he wasn't a film nut.

After I gave up pop culture references I was amazed at how quickly we relaxed and started swopping life stories. It's a cliché but Nate really did have that ability to make me feel like I was the most interesting girl on the planet. He could do for real what Sean had only faked. I couldn't believe he hadn't been snapped up. I prayed he didn't have some awful dark secret.

I almost told Nate about the car crash I'd been in when I was seventeen but I stopped myself.

When there was lull in the conversation, one which was oddly comfortable, I said "You know, I don't think I'll ever really fit at The Agency."

I was hoping Nate would say something like "Oh no, not you, you're perfect for The Agency" but he surprised me by saying

"You definitely don't fit in, Liz. Thank God. You're weird and awkward and one of the most kindly, sincere people I've ever met."

"Oh. I think that's a compliment."

"It is. Do you know the first time I saw you?"

"At the Halloween party?"

"Way before that. It was at a launch party for a new men's body spray. Really cool party. The executive creative director's secretary hadn't hired enough bartenders and the ECD was yelling at her." Nate made a perfect prissy boss face and I giggled. "You jumped behind the bar and started serving drinks, cracking jokes with a big grin on your face. You even walked around with appetizers."

"I've had a lot of experience waitressing," I said. "Too much."

"Whatever. Not everyone would do it. I thought it took a lot of, I don't know what. You're just so...Oh, you know what I mean." Judging by how he was blushing I did. "Are you even a licensed bartender?"

"You'll never know," I said.

"I do love a rebellious girl."

Now it was my turn to blush.

———◆———

Around midnight, we ended up at The Agency. I seem to remember it was because we'd raved about how much we loved the place and Nate wanted to show me the campaign he'd been working on. We'd also decided it was the perfect place to have one last drink. He somehow knew that there was a secret stash of Grey Goose vodka hidden away. A few people were working late on pitches or just hanging out, shooting the breeze, Facebooking, and scrounging up any stray slices of pizza they could get their hands on.

As we walked through the office as steadily as we could manage, I whispered to Nate "You all right there, Superman?" I meant that we should both watch our step but it backfired. Nate picked me up and carried me across the office, taking big strides.

I sighed. "My hero." It felt good to be the person doing something crazy for once.

Nate found the vodka, positioned me so I could open the door to the deck without us being seen and we slipped outside. We made our way to a part of the deck where the neon light didn't reach, and lay down. It was a soft, warm night—perfect for stargazing and passing a bottle back and forth.

I remember telling Nate about my Bikram hot yoga experience. He leapt to his feet and started improvising something called Yoga for Crazy Ad people. We were weak from laughter by the time he finished.

"What do you want to be when you grow up?" I asked Nate.

"Grown up?"

"Very funny. Seriously."

"I really don't know. We're so young, Liz. Do you know what you want to be?"

"No, but I do know it will involve research."

Nate opened his eyes wide, pointed up into the starry sky. "So, from now on, whenever there are people who need your very special kind of help, it won't be a job for plain, ordinary Elizabeth Nelson… It'll be a job for SuperLemon!"

So he did know his Superman. "My hero," I said, patting his right bicep.

I woke up under Nate's leather jacket. He was snoring lightly. Amazingly, it hadn't rained in the night. The sun was rising over the city. Pink was giving way to clear blue. Mount Hood shone in the distance. I was pretty sure nothing had happened between Nate and I, which made the night even more romantic.

When I stood up I realized that we'd fallen asleep directly outside the COO"s office. He was known for getting in to work at a ridiculously early time in the morning. I shivered thinking about what might happen if he'd arrived and seen us asleep on the deck. But it was still only five a.m.

"Nate," I whispered. "Wake up."

He let out a contented sigh, smiled, and stretched. I loved the way that when he opened his blue eyes he wasn't at all surprised to see me, or to find himself on the deck of The Agency as the sun was rising.

"Wow," Nate said, sitting up and yawning. "What a beautiful day. Guess we better get out of here."

Luckily for us no one had thought to lock the door to the deck. The COO wasn't in yet. As we crept past a designer comatose in front of their Mac we placed our empty vodka bottle on his desk before tiptoeing down the stairs. The cleaners were already at work putting a shine on The Agency lobby.

Outside the building, we stood on the sidewalk looking at each other. "Seems a bit crazy to go home doesn't it?" Nate said. "We're not going to get any sleep, are we?"

"Guess not," I said.

"Do you know Beth's?"

"Nope."

"You've never been to Beth's? Boy are you in for a treat. Them omelets aren't world famous for nothing," baby."

As if on cue, my stomach rumbled.

Nate laughed. "I'll take that as a yes."

Minutes later we were rolling through the streets of Seattle, me on the back of Nate's Harley, wearing his leather jacket and spare helmet, my arms around him. It felt so great to be alive on that wonderful, sweetly-scented morning.

After what happened with Sean, I was careful to take things slowly with Nate. I limited our dates to the weekend and we often went out in a group with other creatives from The Agency. They were wild, but underneath the tattoos, nose rings, pierced tongues and dyed hair, they were as ambitious as I was. You couldn't go places at The Agency if you really didn't care about succeeding.

On the weekends that Nate had to work on pitches I would go for at least one long run. I'd always been a runner and the need (or compulsion) to run—fast—had never left me. I ran on the East Side of Seattle, where the best trails were.

I know now that I was not running toward anything. I was running away.

On the East Side, I found the perfect trail for me: serious hills with flat parts in between. The hills made me run hard and the flats gave me release. My body was screaming so I didn't have to.

After an especially tough run, I walked around the beautiful upper-class neighborhoods tucked into the hills. I looked at my favorite houses and dreamed of my life in five to ten years. I pictured barbeques with friends on the lawn and cozy nights with my future family. Strangely, I never imagined being there with Nate, but I suppose that's the funny thing about dreams. They can sometimes predict the future.

A couple of nights a week I went to hot yoga. But during the week, I mostly worked late. The problem was that, no matter how late I worked, I couldn't get to sleep because my mind was racing. I'd lie in bed, desperate for sleep to come, often in pain because I'd eaten too much, too late. I knew enough to know I was out of control. I had a constant feeling of either being too full or too empty. Too much caffeine, too much wine, too tired, too wired, too fast, too slow, too much, too little. I felt exhausted all the time but somehow got through on nervous energy.

But even sleep was exhausting. I had terrible work related anxiety dreams where I'd forgotten to do something. I hadn't been to see a client for an entire project and now had to make a presentation, completely unprepared. I couldn't find the room where we were meeting and, when I got there, I didn't have anything to show. Sometimes I didn't remember what the client looked like and was terrified I would walk right past them. I always woke up immediately after I found the client in my dream and knew I had my presentation prepared. My relief would be replaced by real panic when I realized I only had half an hour before I needed to be at work.

I would walk to The Agency dreading the day and craving my caffeine fix. But when I walked through the doors the adrenaline kicked in and I was back in my happy place. Taking on new projects gave me extra energy. Every night, I was still staring at my screen long after I had promised myself to leave.

It's a strange thing to not know if you are very happy or incredibly depressed. It seemed that I was both, most of the time. I struggled with where to place the blame and what to do about my situation. I couldn't change The Agency and wouldn't dream of leaving. It was my whole life. Except for Rita, all of my friends, my boyfriend, my paycheck and my chance at the kind of future I wanted were there. Logic told me I should stay but something else—my survival instinct, perhaps?—nagged at me to leave. All I could think of was to keep on going.

The end result was that I was running on empty.

———•———

One day, a creative director sent me out of The Agency on an errand. I needed a caffeine fix so I stopped off to pick up a coffee to go. There were mirrors on the walls of the café and behind the counter. I ordered and, while I waited, I zoned out thinking about work. After a few minutes, I saw a reflection in the mirror of a woman giving me the evil eye. She looked really pissed. I was having a terrible day and the last thing I needed was a bitchy stranger staring at me. I got up and walked toward her.

As I got closer, I realized the woman was me. I was looking at my own reflection in the mirror. I felt a crushing sense of defeat. Did I really walk around Seattle looking like this every day? The angry, gaunt, pale woman with bloodshot eyes set in deep, dark hollows didn't look like someone following their dream.

I ran out of the restaurant and burst into tears.

A bikini wax first

I'd been farmed out to our biggest video game client account to work on one of their teenage games. My job was to help the account's strategic planner. I was excited about the project and about working with the planner, who was legendarily "on the ball."

As soon as I was told about the project, I was bursting with what I thought were great ideas. Things got off to a great start at my first meeting with the planner when I met her with some research I'd already prepared. It turned out to be exactly what she needed for a presentation in two weeks.

My job was to persuade teenage girls to keep a journal, recording what it was like to play the game for ten days out of those two weeks, so the planner could use what they wrote in the presentation. We needed all the time we could get.

Nothing happened in the first week of the project. I assumed that we'd shorten the journaling time to make up for this. I was worried that we'd lose the weekend, a time when the girls would have more time to play the game and journal.

I spent a more anxious weekend than usual worrying about how we'd get the research done in time. But on Monday morning the strategist was still preparing. She'd found some girls who were prepared to write the journals and briefed them. I asked if I could help but she refused.

By Wednesday I didn't know how we were going to pull off the research. The strategist tried to scale this down to a day of interviews with the girls on Saturday before the presentation but the client had already heard about the journals, loved the idea, and was expecting to read them.

It looked like the project—and what could have been my big break—was going to be a total failure.

Thursday morning, I headed for my morning catch-up with the strategist expecting to receive my daily dose of "not quite ready yet." On my way down, I was pulled into a meeting on a different project. After this, I decided that the strategist would email me if she'd made any progress on the project that day and got on with something else.

Friday was the last working day before the client flew in for the presentation. I went to meet the strategist with no idea what to expect. She was smiling and happy and I assumed she'd found a way to rescue the situation.

"OK, Liz, show me what you've got," she said. "I can't wait."

I was completely confused. What on earth was she talking about? "Um, what would you like to see?"

"The journals, silly. We need to hustle and I've got to work on the presentation over the weekend."

"Oh. Did you finish them? That's great. I can go through them with you."

"No, Liz," the strategist said, looking me straight in the eye. "You sent out the journals. Now we need to analyze them and put the findings into our presentation."

I almost fainted. I had no memory other than the strategist telling me the journals were "almost ready."

The strategist insisted she'd given me the journals days before. I couldn't think of anything to say in my defense. If she was right, there wasn't anything.

Finally, she said "I can't believe you dropped the ball on this one, Liz. I'm sorry, but I can't rely on you. I won't need your help over the weekend."

I wanted to scream "You never gave them to me, you crazy bitch! You're the one who fucked up and you won't admit it." Instead I stammered "I'm so sorry" a couple more times until the strategist turned back to her screen and waved me away.

Furious and humiliated, I locked myself in the bathroom and tried to remember if the strategist had given me the journals but I knew she hadn't. I decided to talk to the head of strategy but the strategist beat me to it. When I got back to my desk there was an email from the head of strategy asking me to go see him.

I realized right then I should have gone to see him immediately after my meeting with the planner.

When I told my side of the story to the head of strategy I was almost in tears. Tears of rage. I poured everything out as I sat taking deep breaths. He gave me a little smile and patted my hand.

"I'm sorry you had a bad experience," he said. "But if you want to make your mark at The Agency you need to really focus on the work at hand, even when the strategists aren't."

I opened my mouth to say something but realized that, right then, I didn't have the words. The planner had saved herself by lying about me. She'd built the lie by accusing me, convincing herself she was right—which was either insane or smart. And I had learned a major lesson. When it comes to work, people usually save themselves.

All that day, my mind didn't stop whirling. I kept asking myself a question I couldn't answer: Was I really putting everything into my work or just going through the motions?

By 6 p.m. that evening I couldn't sit at my desk any longer. Leaving it in careful disarray, as if I'd only stepped away for a minute, I left.

It was weird to step out into daylight. When I got home I had no idea what to do with myself. I desperately wanted to speak to Nate but I knew he would be working until the early hours of the morning on a new business pitch. The Agency had been doing a lot of pitching recently and Nate had been involved with most of the pitches. This was great because it meant that The Agency trusted him to come up with the goods. But he wasn't a good loser, and we'd been losing more pitches than we won recently.

When I got home I knocked on Rita's door but there was no answer. There was no way I could sit still in my own room or do some sort of chore like straightening things up or doing my laundry. The only thing I could think of was to run.

I drank Mike's Hard Lemonade for a sugar rush, put on my running gear and headed for the East Side. I tried not to run after dark but I didn't care. I welcomed a confrontation with something real and nasty that I could defeat.

I also thought that if I could just run to the end of the hills, the end of the woods, the end of my energy, everything would somehow be all right. I would finally know what I was doing. I would break out of the pit I was in, and be content. In the meantime, I would keep running.

But running didn't help. Once the sugar rush wore off, my timing felt all wrong. I couldn't find my rhythm, couldn't get to that place where thinking stopped. To lose myself, I ran further than I ever had before. I ran until the hills ended. It was as if I'd run to the edge of a video game, where the familiar images end and nothing begins. Where the houses got fewer and fewer and the tree tops covered up the sky. I ran until I hit a dead end—a cul-de-sac of beautiful houses.

I was empty. But, unlike before, this wasn't a good feeling. I was frightened. It was dark now. And I was desperately cold and tired.

———•———

"Earth to Liz. Earth to Liz. Come in Liz."

Rita's voice in my ear snapped me out of my trance. I looked down at my phone on the table next to a cold cup of coffee. It was 8 am on Friday morning and I wasn't even dressed. My mind felt empty but not in a good way. I wondered if something had broken inside me.

"You OK, Liz?"

Getting the words out was an effort but, after what seemed like forever, I said "I'm fine. A little tired is all." My voice sounded like it came from very far away.

"Sorry to say this but you don't look too great. Why don't you stay home today?"

"I have to go into work." I began to stand up but it felt like someone was banging nails into my thighs. I sat down again. "Whoops, think I overdid it with the running last night."

"Seriously, Liz," Rita said, "You look terrible. I really don't think you should go to work today. Want me to call in sick for you?"

"No," I said. But my mind had started turning over the possibility of going back to bed. I couldn't remember the last time I'd taken a sick day. It had certainly never happened at The Agency. "If you call in for me they'll know I'm faking."

I looked down at my phone. My fingers strayed to the touchpad. I looked up at Rita. I wondered if she had some sort of ulterior motive for persuading me not to go into work but all I could see in her face was real concern. She covered my hand with hers and squeezed it. And I burst into tears.

"Let me call them," Rita said. "Please."

I went to work.

———◆———

This time I woke up to the sound of Rita tapping on my door. For a split-second I had no idea where or even who I was. I must have slept so deeply. "Come in," I said, my eyes still closed. My voice sounded croaky but a little bit stronger.

Rita sat down on the edge of my bed. I opened my eyes. She handed me a mug with steam coming out of the top of it.

I peered into the mug and saw a yellowy-white liquid. "What is it?"

"It's called golden milk."

"And...?"

"It's a mixture of turmeric and coconut milk. It's an anti-inflammatory. Really good for sore muscles and, I don't know, plenty of other stuff. Honest, it's sooo good for you."

I made a face. "Really," Rita said. "It's awesome. Try some."

I took a sip. It wasn't so bad but I couldn't say it was good either. I just hoped it would help me.

"Listen, Liz," Rita said. "I have to go out now."

"What's the time?"

"Nine."

"In the morning?" I sat upright in bed, almost spilling golden milk down myself. "I'm late for work."

Rita smiled. "Yes, nine in the morning but it's Saturday. You've been out cold for 14 hours."

"Wow. Where are you going?"

"Bikini wax time girl."

"Hot date?"

"Looks that way, yep."

One of the things I adored about Rita was the way she was perfectly happy to contradict herself. She was as feminist as they come but also ultra-feminine. As she put it to me once, "No man—or woman—is going to tell me I can't remove my lady hair. Us Indian women have been doing it for centuries. So you could say that by having a bikini wax I'm honoring my heritage. In my case, though, we're talking Brazilian all the way baby. And I like it. That's really why I do it. I like the feeling. And I kind of like the pain too."

"I don't," I said. "Luckily I'm as blonde as you're dark so I don't have to do it that often."

"When did you last go?"

"Um, no idea."

"Wanna come with me?"

My first reaction was to say no and stay in bed. But I was so grateful to Rita and it had been ages since I'd just hung out with another girl who had no connection to work or any of the other serious things in my life. I wanted to be pleasantly mindless for a while, take a time out from reality. My real life would all start again tomorrow. Meanwhile, today was today and I might as well enjoy it. If you could call having a bikini wax pleasure.

"Sure. Why not?"

For the second time that day I woke up to Rita's concerned face hovering over me. This time it was joined by that of the exquisite Korean girl who had been waxing my bikini line. They looked worried but also fascinated.

"That's the first time this has ever happened," the Korean girl explained, her perfectly drawn eyebrows raised up almost to her hairline.

"What?" I asked, sitting straight up. "Is there something wrong?"

"You fell asleep again," Rita said. "While you were having your lady hair ripped out! Scary. A wake-up call, girl. You've been working way too hard."

"That's the truth," the Korean girl said, nodding. "I'll call you ladies a cab."

"I'm okay." I struggled to sit up.

"No one who falls asleep when they're having their bikini line waxed is okay," the Korean girl said.

Rita sighed. "That is also the truth."

Rita cancelled her hot date. We spent the day lying side by side on her bed telling stories about work. All of her stories were about clients with terrible depression and anxiety disorders. I think she was trying to make me feel better. Every time she told me a truly miserable story, I countered with something funny. Like the story of a client getting us all kicked out of a strip club.

After we'd gone a few minutes without talking, and without me feeling pressured to fill the silence, Rita asked "And how's it going with Nate?"

"Great. We're going to see Sleater Kinney next week." I paused. "Nate's so creative and so are all his friends. It's awesome. I just wish I was more creative. More like them."

"Sure. But it's fun to date guys you know it won't work out with. Anyway, it doesn't seem like he's the kind to dump you so you can just leave him when you're ready. I think it's Prosecco time, don't you?"

Rita rolled off the bed and headed for the kitchen, leaving me somewhat shocked, staring at the Bollywood movie playing silently on her giant TV. How could she think my creative, motor-cycle riding Clark Kent look-alike was anything but a home run? I felt so proud of myself that I'd paired up with someone who was interesting, cute, and normal while still being exciting.

I was still trying to process what Rita had said when she came back with the Prosecco and two glasses. "Not quite chilled. But that's how we like it, right?" Then she saw my face. "Maybe I spoke too soon about Nate, Liz. Forget it."

She filled my glass and then hers. We tapped them together in a toast. "What about your love life?" I asked.

Rita took a sip of her Prosecco. "I wanted to talk with you about that. My parents and sisters are coming to Seattle for a family gathering next week. I'd like you to come with me so they can meet you and see the relationship we've built."

"Sure."

"Great. My parents are a little old fashioned and have never met a lesbian before so don't be offended by their reaction."

"Excuse me? You told your parents I'm a lesbian?"

Rita smiled sweetly. "No Liz. I would be introducing us as a couple. Which insinuates you are a lesbian. A lady chaser, if you will."

"Do you think I'm gay? Is that why you said it wouldn't work out with me and Nate?"

"Do you think you're gay, Liz?"

I stared at her, stunned. Why was a psychologist asking me that question as if she already knew the answer? Rita just fixed her huge eyes on me and waited. She took a sip of her Prosecco and then exploded in a fit of giggles, spitting her drink all over herself and the bed. She laughed until the Prosecco started coming out of her nose and then she screamed that it was burning. I tried to laugh but she'd really got me good.

When she'd gotten her breath back, Rita said "Sorry Liz," but I knew she was delighted with herself.

All I could manage was "I find it so sad that you use your powers for evil and not good. So sad."

Rita shrugged. She dabbed her streaming eyes, blew her nose. "Actually, I would like you to come. My family is always asking to meet my friends. The lesbian thing isn't entirely a joke."

I moved away from her on the bed. "Don't worry, Liz. I'm not a lesbian. The thing is, I don't want an arranged marriage and the way my dating habits are going I'm going to end up with a blonde haired blue-eyed guy. If I told them I was a lesbian and then made a joke out of it, maybe it would soften them up for when I turn up with someone who's really going to rock their world."

"I'm your family's worst case scenario then?"

"A blond lesbian? For sure."

"OK," I said. "Let's do it."

I went to work on Monday, rested and full of optimism. By mid-morning, however, I noticed that no one was meeting my eye or stopping to have the kind of catch-up chat that usually happened. I thought it was something I'd done. Then I saw that no one was meeting anyone else's eye. There were no loud conversations or bursts of laugher. Only whispers.

Something was up but I didn't know what.

Around lunchtime Nate came around. He looked pale and distracted as he sat on the edge of my desk. "Wanna go out for something to eat?" he asked. "Get some fresh air?"

This was a first for him; we never left The Agency at lunch-time. The most we ever did was eat in the café together. "I'd love to," I said. "But I'm too busy."

Kat appeared and shot Nate a look that could have meant anything. He slipped off my desk, leaned forward and, without moving his mouth, whispered "Layoffs. Later."

Now everything made sense. "What's this about layoffs, Kat?" I asked.

"Keep your voice down," she hissed.

"Is it true?" I hissed back.

"Yes. We lost the Sucre Soda account. They'll be letting people go at the end of next week."

I breathed a sigh of relief. "So we're safe then?"

"Not exactly. This is the perfect excuse for them to do what they call 'clean house.' By which they mean anyone who doesn't," she made air quotation marks, 'add value.'"

"We add value don't we?"

Kat sighed and smiled. "We think we do. But we don't know if they think we do. Or if they think we did but have decided we don't. Or if they still think we do but they can't afford to have us doing something that doesn't make money for them. I've been here seven years Liz and I've seen seven rounds of layoffs."

"You mean this happens every year?" I squeaked.

"Keep your voice down. And yes. It happens every year. But their logic for choosing who's cut loose when they clean house has never made any sense to me. It's just the nature of the beast. So I really don't know, Liz. It doesn't help that those hungry bastards at Electric Phonebooth took a giant bite out of our sportswear account. All we can do is keep working."

I sat at my desk thinking that I really was too nice for advertising. I had no idea how I would get through the next couple of days. But it did give a focus for all my worries, so much so that the fear that I was going to lose control and run screaming out of The Agency disappeared completely. Now I wanted to stay there forever. I resolved to keep my head down and hope for the best.

And then I remembered something.

———•———

"I'll see what I can do," Brook said. "But you should know, Liz, it's probably too late to find Nate a place on another account. And it's not really what I do."

"Thank you so much, Brook," I said. "Anything you can do will help. Nate does great work. He's worked on so many pitches. And the work he does on the Sucre Soda account has been awesome."

"I think I recruited Nate. He was pretty talented as I recall. I know he does great work. I'll set up a meeting with him. But you need to be aware, Liz, that once The Agency makes up its mind to let people go, whatever the reason, it doesn't usually change its mind."

I smiled, fought back tears, and went back to my desk. All day I felt dread rising up in me until I thought it would burst out of my ears.

That night, oddly enough, I slept deeply and, the next morning, I couldn't remember any of my dreams. It felt like something had been taken out of my hands.

———•———

It all began first thing on Tuesday. I was at my desk even earlier than usual, around seven. I opened my inbox with a sinking feeling, expecting to see a message telling me to report to The Cave, where the Executive Creative Directors—ECDs—who were doing the letting go had installed themselves, but there was nothing. I felt like I'd won the lottery until I remembered I had the rest of the week to go.

Brook came in a little after me. Although she smiled at me when she passed, she looked terribly sad and defeated. Brook's job was to recruit the best creatives by promising them a glittering future at The Agency. In the previous few weeks more than five of the brilliant people Brook had enticed to The Agency had been let go one by one. There was just no work for them. One of these, a copywriter, had moved with his family from New York only a month before.

I'd never been let go in my life. I had no idea how it might feel, other than terrible. I couldn't decide whether it was better not to know what it was like or to have been through the experience before and be prepared.

I came back from a meeting around 10:30 and Kat said "It's started. They're emailing people to go to the Cave. So far Kevin and Brandon have gone in and not come back." Kevin and Brandon were account people. If any agency is shrinking, they're usually the first to go.

When I first started at The Agency, the Cave seemed like a cool, offbeat idea that I used to love telling people about, especially after I'd survived my own visit back when I worked on the Escalate sports account.

When The Agency was growing and had money, the Cave was amusing. Now it seemed ridiculous to the point of grotesque. Can you imagine losing your job perched on a soft pebble covered in fake bird poo while water trickled down a tower of pebbles? And what did the ECDs think? Were they embarrassed at humiliating people? Did they secretly think it was funny? Either way, the thought of being called into the Cave again filled me with terror.

The fact that the door to the Cave was always open made it even worse. If someone being let go lost it in the Cave we would all hear everything. I felt a bit like a gawker at a car accident because I wanted to shut out everything that was happening but I also wanted to know.

As it turned out, the drama began for me a little bit closer to home.

At around 12, a personal assistant to one of the ECDs appeared at the desk of a producer who worked near me. Her face was white, made even more so by her black clothes. She leant over him and whispered in his ear.

"NO!" he shouted, swiveling on his chair to look up at her and making her, me and everyone else around him jump out of our skin. "I have work to do. If they want to talk to me, they can schedule a meeting not just send me an email out of the blue."

I snuck a look at the producer's face. It was red with rage but in his eyes I saw pure fear and impotence. He knew making a scene was only delaying the inevitable but he was going to do it anyway. The PA said something to him in a low voice, which outraged him even more. "I SAID NO!" he bellowed.

The PA straightened up, shrugged her shoulders and stalked away. Although her face was a mask, she was trembling. I felt so sorry for the producer but I also thought the way he'd treated the PA was wrong. She was only doing her job.

A few minutes later, the most senior ECD appeared at the producer's desk. This guy was completely calm and in control. He smiled at the producer and said "Hey, how are you doing? Can I have a word in private?"

The request was put so reasonably that the producer had no choice but to stand up. The ECD pointed in the direction of the conference room on our floor and they walked side by side towards it. The producer wasn't going to go first, like a condemned man to an execution, but he wasn't going to follow like a sheep. The door to the conference room was, however, only wide enough for one person. I'm sure I wasn't the only person watching to see what would happen.

In the end, the ECD opened the door, stepped to one side and invited the producer into the conference room. By that point, the producer knew that the ECD didn't really care whether he appeared to lose face or not. He'd already won.

This didn't stop the producer from making a horrific noise in the conference room. He started out by swearing at the top of his voice. Then he begged. Then he cried. And all the while the ECD kept his own voice low and measured.

I realized I had to pee very badly but I couldn't get up and go. I wished with all my heart I was on another floor. Most of all, though, I wished I'd had time to become one of those people every company has who is never let go because nobody quite knows what they do.

Fifteen minutes later the drama ended. The producer walked out of the conference room utterly broken. The ECD followed him out, his suntanned face Zen calm and inscrutable. Every single one of us stared at our computers as the producer—a guy we'd all joked and laughed with, who had been a friend to some of us—walked past his desk and out the door.

I didn't know what I thought about what had just happened. What had happened to the producer was horrible and humiliating but, in a way, he'd brought it on himself by not simply bowing gracefully to the inevitable like everyone else had. And although I thought there was something noble in the way the ECD had handled the situation without getting angry or emotional himself, he looked like he enjoyed exercising his power over the producer.

After the producer and the ECD had gone, I put my headphones and focused on my computer, shutting out everything that was going on around me. But I couldn't shut out the awful tension. All the drama had completely killed my appetite.

I stayed at my desk all day and didn't eat a thing. People from my floor were called into the Cave. Some were asked to finish out the day. Others—like the producer—left immediately. I didn't know which was best: to make a clean break or to spend the day with people whose jobs were safe while yours had vanished. Either way seemed terribly cruel.

Around 10:30 that night I went to look for Nate, to see if he wanted to go out for a drink or something. I prayed that he was still at his desk. He was and I breathed a huge sigh of relief. He stood up, gave me a quick hug and a peck on the cheek. I looked into his eyes and saw fear. If he was let go it would be a major blow to his career and to our relationship. The only place he could go to move up the ladder, or at least maintain his current status, would be to an agency out of state. I had no idea what I would do if that happened. I'd tried not to think about it.

But it seemed like Nate was safe for today at least. He would be working on a pitch until he didn't know when. "Tomorrow night, babe, when this is all over and I've been promoted, we'll go out and paint the town," he said in his best Big Easy drawl.

I hoped he was right. I kissed him on top of the head. "By Odin's Beard," I whispered.

A couple of Nate's friends rolled up, a writer and art director team, and asked us if we wanted to go to dinner. He told them he couldn't leave. They understood why better than anyone. I was so hungry by that time that I thought I was going to faint. So I went with them.

We chose a restaurant off the beaten track, where there was no chance of us bumping into anyone from The Agency. We ordered large quantities of food and a couple of bottles of wine, which we all started guzzling right away.

I was the first one to bring up the subject of the layoffs. "I counted up to fourteen," I said. "Is it done?"

"No," the writer said. "I heard they're laying off thirty people altogether so it'll be all day tomorrow and maybe part of Friday."

"Funny," I said, "I've heard that Friday afternoon is the best time to lay people off. Sorry, I didn't mean to say funny."

"Maybe," the writer said. "But thirty people would make for a lot of Friday afternoons, wouldn't it?"

As we got drunker we became sillier. I began to feel guilty that we were laughing and joking while Nate was in fear for his job. I left the writer and art director, both very drunk, and went back to The Agency. I turned off my desk lamp and then went up to Nate's floor. I was going to see how he was doing and ask him if he wanted to come home with me but when I saw him hunched over his computer in a world of his own I turned and left.

———•———

All that night I dreamed I was lost in a place I couldn't find my way out of. Sometimes it was The Agency. At other points in my dream it was my college. As soon as I figured out where I was, my dreamscape mutated into somewhere else entirely.

By 5 am I was showered and I'd had my breakfast. I was at the grocery store when it opened and bought snacks, something for lunch and dinner. I was determined to only leave my desk if it was absolutely necessary. I would be a model employee. Obviously, this was ridiculous. The list of people being let go had already been drawn up. If I was going to go, that was that. But I thought—and this shows you how little I knew—that someone might have been crossed off the let-go-list for good behavior or a sudden, amazing burst of great work. I would be the one to be kicked out in their place.

I didn't leave my desk even to pee all that Thursday. I kept my eyes grimly focused on my computer. I wasn't alone in doing this. All around me, people were glued to their chairs. The office was as quiet as the grave. At around four, Kat told me she'd heard that the culling was finished. I should have felt intensely relieved but all I felt was a terrible headache. My first thought was to find out about Nate.

I called his phone and left a voicemail. I sent a text. I even emailed him. But I got nothing back. I was sure he would have told me if he'd been let go so I wasn't too worried. Perhaps he was celebrating being kept on, or even promoted, I thought.

An email popped into my inbox. We were all asked to meet in The Agency auditorium at five. The auditorium was in the center of the building on the second floor. It was where The Agency talked to us about anything significant. Back when I'd started, there had been so many of us we spilled out onto the stars and watched from the floors above. Now, though we barely filled it.

We waited in silence. The atmosphere was sullen, almost angry. I looked for Nate but couldn't find him. Still, I hoped. Perhaps he'd been allowed to go home. After all, he'd probably worked on that pitch the night before until the sun came up.

The head ECD, the guy who'd personally handled the culling of the producer, took the stage. It looked like the events of the past few days hadn't affected him at all. "Thank you for coming, people," he said. Even though we'd had no choice.

He dropped his voice an octave or two, so it oozed sincerity. "It's been a tough few days, people. For all of us. As many of you know, The Agency has lost a fair bit of business and we've had to adjust our size accordingly." He paused, shook his head, looked down at the floor. "It's sad," he said. Then he looked up, grinned, showing perfect teeth. He made his voice upbeat and defiant. "But you know what, people. That's the business we're in. This, people, this is rock and roll! Am I right?"

This statement was perfectly judged. The mood among those of us who hadn't been kicked out of paradise changed instantly. Immediately, we started to think of ourselves as the elite again, the chosen. A red velvet rope had been placed around The Agency again. We were inside and everyone else, even our departed former comrades, band members or whatever you wanted to call them, were outside.

The sense of relief I felt at not being kicked out of Valhalla, at being one of the chosen, was so strong it made me dizzy. But another feeling was growing inside me, something I couldn't quite name yet.

And where was Nate?

PART TWO

OPPORTUNITY

The green light

"So why don't we start your research with the CBRE office and our own employees, Liz? What do you say to that?"

Wouter Oosting, CBRE's Senior Director of Workspace Strategies and Design, leaned back in his chair and smiled. I knew he was serious but also that I was being tested.

"Sure. Great. Why not?" I said, amazed at how calm my voice sounded.

"Excellent. I'll leave it to you to write a proposal. But now, please excuse me, I'm already late for my next meeting." Wouter stood up. I started to do the same but before I could make it to my feet he'd taken my hand in one of his, shaken it and was out the door of the CBRE meeting room.

I was left looking at the last slide of my PowerPoint presentation. It read, "Thank you for your time."

It was spring 2015. Six years after I'd left The Agency.

———◆———

I'd begun approaching companies to do a longitudinal, or long-term, study pretty much from the second I knew I wanted to research employee health.

From the very beginning, my eyes were focused on consultancies like CBRE. I wanted them to be able to use my findings to advise their clients as soon as the research was completed. For reasons deeply rooted in my experiences with The Agency, I needed to believe my work would result in real, lasting change.

I had begun to realize that ground-breaking scientific research was not put into practice as often as it should have been. Or, if it was, the application was only partial. So I needed to find someone, a sponsor, who believed in making real change as much as I did.

To do this they had to understand what I was trying to do.

For most of the consultancies I spoke with, the concept of a healthy office existed at the basic level of pool tables or free healthy snacks in the cafeteria. These things are nice, but they don't make the profound difference to office culture I believed was possible.

Wouter grasped the real goal of my research right away.

———◆———

After I made my pitch to Wouter at our first meeting, he said "You know, Liz, your timing couldn't be better. We've been wanting to make our own office environment healthier for a while. The problem we've found is that, although plenty of people claim they can improve productivity by creating healthier environments or office ecosystems, they can't offer hard proof that it's possible. People tell us they can increase our employee productivity by twenty percent, which means doing five days' work in four, but they can't provide the evidence to support their claims. Can you?"

"To be honest," I said, "I don't know."

Wouter smiled. "Nor do I," he said. "But we can try to find out. And the data you collect in your research will give us the scientific proof—or not, as the case may be."

Wouter later told me that it was the connection I'd made between collecting scientific data about employee health and office environments and what CBRE wanted to achieve that really sold him on my project. He'd immediately grasped the fact that it was the data we gathered that would guide our next steps.

Although he's not as much of a "techie" as I am, technology plays a big part in Wouter's vision. We both believe that in the future, technology will be far more of a catalyst, taking us to the next level as humans: man and machine together. This is consistent with the way I see wearable technology.

The fact that I proposed to gather hard data was the difference between my pitch and the ones he and CBRE had heard before. As he put it, I had, without knowing it, met CBRE's "need connection."

———•———

When I met Wouter, he'd been thinking about how to make offices healthier for some time. He'd been a successful real estate consultant for many years and his role had always been to create high performance, high efficiency workplaces. Now, though, he was shifting away from this priority and considering the people who worked in offices as well as the human environment the offices provided.

Wouter was among the first to realize that, for a number of reasons, it is now vital for organizations to rethink the way they see offices.

As companies shift production to countries with lower hourly rates, and as a growing amount of what we define as work is being digitized, companies are employing fewer people. These people are increasingly hired for qualities they possess that can't be replicated by machines or less skilled people. They are what Wouter calls "radical workers."

Radical workers are often exceptionally creative, empathetic or open-minded people. They're highly sought after and they know it. Any organization that wants to hire and keep them has to offer a work environment that's appealing and enables them to thrive. Organizations that focus on social innovation in their offices are more likely to be successful at recruiting and retaining highly desirable radical workers.

In this case, social innovation—meeting the social needs of employees (defining "social" as factors that take the needs of people into account, anything from a healthy environment to human connection and promoting self-esteem)—is all about working conditions.

This was the thinking at The Agency but it was only half-right. We were offered a beautiful and stimulating environment to work in. But underneath, The Agency was really a machine for getting the best out of people without taking into account the human cost and the long-term effects of this on the agency itself. In the pursuit of excellence, people were addicted to the notion that advertising had to be seen as rock and roll: unbalanced, unscientific and with only winners and losers. We were encouraged to believe that this was what stimulated out-standing creativity

For most companies, 90% of their cost is spent on employee salaries, expenses, bonuses and so on. Just 1% goes into utilities and 9% on workspaces.[1] The company's emphasis on productivity is necessary to recoup their investment.

This is why it makes total sense to invest in optimizing employee brain function and physical health and make people happier and more productive for longer periods of time. Putting employees, especially radical workers, in an environment scientifically optimized to keep them healthy and happy is likely to have a significant impact on an organization's bottom line.

And when an organization has a reputation for taking care of its employees, while simultaneously doing great work, it will inevitably attract radical workers. Offices play a huge role in this. They must become even more appealing to employees precisely because they're increasingly irrelevant. Many of us rarely go into them, working at home or in a variety of other settings. We work as we move through cities, connecting and interacting in locations geared up to enable us to work flexibly. When we do go to the office, it needs to provide the same comfortable environment as our own home.

But, although we might be working in bustling cafés, hotel lobbies, airports or wherever, we're often working alone or in small groups. Call it a "creative space" or whatever you like, there still is no substitute for a place where people in an organization come together, at least for part of the time, to build a sense of shared purpose and culture.

For Wouter and I, the question was and is "How can we really unlock employees' potential?"

When we first met, either he or I asked, "Why don't we treat employees like professional athletes?"

1   Cited in Browning B. (2012) "The Economics of Biophilia: Why designing with nature in mind makes sense". Available: http://www.interfacereconnect.com/ wp-content/uploads/2012/11/The-Economics-of-Biophilia_Terrapin-BrightGreen-2012e_1.pdf. (Accessed May 30, 2017)

We wondered why athletes consider their mental health a crucial part of their physical performance but the work that employees do with their minds is separated pretty much entirely from their physical health. Why do organizations still engage in the kind of short term thinking that causes them to work people to the point of exhaustion and office them in unhealthy environments with little light and bad nutrition, including plenty of coffee and sugar, to "help" them power through incredibly long days?

Wouter believed change began with "self-repairing." He'd been at a presentation in Los Angeles given by Integrative Medicine Pioneer Deepak Chopra. Wouter had studied Chopra's idea of self-healing—literally our ability to heal ourselves—and was now thinking about how to enable people to self-heal. Or, as he put it, self-repair, in an office environment.

I was not convinced that it was simply a case of people healing themselves. Rates of burnout are increasing to a frightening level even in countries like The Netherlands, which has one of the highest standards of living and individual health awareness in the world. Many people know how to stay healthy and avoid burning out but they still damage their physical and mental health in the name of work. I believed change had to start with the whole ecosystem in which people lived and worked.

So, if you could convince organizations to incorporate the notion of self-repair, starting with itself as a whole and working downwards to include the individual office environment, you might be on to something. Self-repairing people could influence office environments. Healthy groups of workers or departments could influence other groups, and so on.

If organizations like CBRE invest in making their employees healthier and more satisfied, it's highly likely the employees would become more productive, and therefore make more money for the company. As Wouter says, it's a "ping-ping situation," AKA "Win-Win."

———◆———

That first afternoon after meeting Wouter, I left the CBRE offices utterly inspired. If everything worked out the way I hoped it would, we could change the game and help millions of people work in a far better, healthier way. I was ready to fight to make it happen, and I had the feeling Wouter was, too.

Although his official title was and is Senior Director Workplace Strategies & Design, Wouter was known as the company's dreamer. I was incredibly fortunate to be put in touch with CBRE, the world's largest real estate firm. And I was unbelievably lucky to meet Wouter Oosting.

Wouter may be a visionary but he is grounded in science and research. Which was one of the reasons why he grasped the logic behind my PhD research project and, without saying anything to me, immediately saw its potential for CBRE's business.

But even if Wouter understood what I was doing right away, we still had a long way to go before I would be allowed to do my research in CBRE's offices.

———◆———

After our meeting, I stepped out into an Amsterdam evening that was almost warm. As I waited for the traffic lights to change, I couldn't help but remember how I'd felt when I'd finally been offered a place at The Agency. I was just as thrilled now.

The traffic lights turned to green and I crossed over.

PART THREE

RESEARCH

Burnout returns on the wings of opportunity

Picture this. You work in an office of 450 people. The office is a well-oiled machine, ultra-efficient and geared to meeting challenging targets day in and day out. One day a researcher appears, as if she's been beamed in from Mars.

The researcher seems somehow to have convinced your bosses to let her carry out a seven-month survey involving you and around a third of the people in your office. But no one has a clue as to what the research is meant to prove.

In those seven months, you're subjected to all kinds of surveys and experiments. You wear a thing on your wrists that sends data back to the weird researcher although you have no idea precisely why. The researcher interviews you a few times and you often catch sight of her watching you with a strange glint in her eye. No one will tell you why she's doing what she's doing. All you know is that it has something to do with health.

How would you feel?

———◆———

I really sympathized with the people at CBRE who were desperate to know the results of my research. I did my best to keep a poker face when they casually asked me if things were going well. The truth was I was absolutely thrilled with what I was finding out. I couldn't wait to share the results. But I was still nervous.

Any researcher will tell you that when we're involved in a project we're in our own little bubble. We record, read results, analyze and discover and that's it. One of the big challenges is to remember that although we're gathering amazing insights, we're working with real people, not simply research "subjects." After spending all that time analyzing data, it comes as a quite a shock when we're asked to present our research findings in front of an audience of other living, breathing human beings.

I always think of it as a bit like when the Invisible Woman from the Fantastic Four materializes in front of people and they realize she's been watching them and knows exactly what they're doing. It's a bit creepy. But, of course, she's a superhero so she's on the side of good.

I was happily working through my research findings when I got a call from Wouter.

"Hey Liz," Wouter said. "How's it going?"

"Good," I replied. Wouter's tone of voice made me feel like he was going to say something important but I had no idea what.

"You know there's a real buzz building up around your research, don't you?"

"I know. It's great. People are asking me how it's going all the time and they're fishing for answers."

Wouter laughed. "That's to be expected. But the buzz I'm talking about is coming from a bit higher up." He paused. "Listen, Liz. Somehow the people at CoreNet have heard about what we're doing and they want us to speak at their European fall conference."

"What's CoreNet?"

"They're a non-profit, all about making corporate real estate as good as it can be. Hugely respected. We're a member of the organization, naturally. Speaking at their conference is a massive honor. And it's great for the project."

"Fantastic. When is the conference?"

Wouter paused again, chuckled. "It's in September."

"But it's July now!"

"I know. So, you think you can get something together by then?"

I knew I couldn't hesitate. "Yes."

"Excellent, Liz. I knew you could do it. Actually it's we. There's rather a lot for me to do too. I'll be in touch. Enjoy the rest of your day."

"Bye Wouter," I said.

I sat looking at my phone for a while, stunned. I had just 40 days to finish the analysis and write the presentation. It didn't occur to me to ask Wouter how CoreNet had just happened to hear about my research.

I learned an incredibly valuable lesson while I was racing to finish my research, write up the results and prepare the presentation for CoreNet. I began working crazy hours and almost burned out all over again. But this time I could adjust my behavior and, a fascinating thing for a researcher, have the opportunity to test whether what I recommended for other people actually worked on myself.

What I learned was that, unless we're very careful, it's extremely easy for any ambitious person who wants to do excellent work for whatever reasons to push themselves to the point where their mental and physical health are at risk.

Fortunately, I was in control of my working environment, not subject to peer pressure, and a little older and wiser. I pulled back from the edge.

———•———

When we did our presentation at the CoreNet conference, all I could see were rows of faces. This was the largest audience I'd ever presented to and I was terrified. I tried not to look at individuals in case they yawned or did something or other that undermined my confidence. It felt good to have Wouter up there with me though.

Our presentation was organized into three parts. The first was a trend analysis that attempted to predict the future of offices, presented by Hannah Hahn, Global Workplace Innovation Manager at CBRE. I presented the research design and results and talked about the implications for organizations. Wouter finished things off with a presentation on the business case for healthier offices.

I was so "in the moment" when I gave my presentation that I really couldn't remember anything I said. Nor could I concentrate on Wouter's presentation. I was amazed, though, when people started coming out of the audience and up onto the stage to congratulate us.

"You guys pulled off the best event of the conference," said a tall, intense young man as he pumped my hand and then Wouter's. "That was great."

I couldn't speak. I just smiled. "Thank you," Wouter said.

"Seriously," the young man said. "I mean it."

Wouter turned to me and started to say something when he was interrupted by a British guy who slapped him on the back and said, "That was marvelous you two. We need to talk about how we do this in the London office. I'll call you tomorrow, Wouter, and we'll set up a meeting."

I looked at Wouter. He smiled. "Well done, Liz."

I stayed at The Agency for two years after that horrible day. In those two years, I threw myself into work and helped build the research team into a recognized research department. Once a year, there were rounds of layoffs and I never got used to them. Nor did Brook, who remained my best friend at The Agency.

Every time there was a layoff, Brook was the only person who said what she really thought. I was standing next to her at one Agency bash not long after a layoff when she quietly gave the CEO a piece of her mind. "The people you let go trusted me," she said. "They came to The Agency from all over the world—Europe, Asia, Australia, South America—and not just the US. I convinced them they would be safe here."

The CEO started to open his mouth but Brook cut him off. "When you get rid of them, they have to sell their houses if they've managed to be able to buy one. If they have kids, they've got to change schools. They'll have to move to another state if they want a decent career in advertising. And you tell the rest of us 'It's only rock and roll.' I don't know exactly why you lay people off—actually, I've got a pretty good idea—but it sure as shit ain't rock and roll."

Turning to me, Brook grinned. "Shall we dance, Liz?"

I've never felt more proud than when Brook slipped her arm

through mine, led me out onto the dance floor and we both danced like maniacs. There's nothing better than when someone you admire likes you back.

At the end of the evening, we were sitting with our aching feet up on chairs, sharing a bottle of champagne. "You really are too nice for this, Liz," Brook said.

"You always say that. I'm trying not to be."

"Why?"

"I want to make something of myself."

"There must be better ways."

"Maybe there are. But I haven't found one."

"Keep looking, baby. Keep looking."

———•———

Like all of us back then, a lot of my life happened on Facebook. I never really got my real life outside of work going in Seattle. Rita was my only flesh and blood friend in the city who didn't work for The Agency.

For some reason that I never quite figured out, I never told anyone at The Agency when it was my birthday. On the morning of my 26th birthday, I was easing myself into work by Facebooking when I received a message from a guy called Nicholas. As they say, my heart skipped a beat.

I'd last run into Nicholas in a Denver bar the week before I moved to Seattle. He was walking in as I was heading out. His astonishingly hideous Hawaiian shirt made him hard to miss. He said he was wearing it to celebrate having finished his MBA. I almost believed him. Somehow or other we fell into an intense conversation. He forgot to get a drink and I forgot to leave for two hours.

It turned out that this was the last week in Denver for both of us. Nicholas was heading to The Netherlands. His American accent had been hiding the fact that he was actually half Dutch. When we gave each other a hug at the end of the night, I walked away thinking, "Oh well, Liz. Could have been the one that got away." Which just goes to show how wrong you can be.

We stayed in touch for maybe six months but that was it. Our new lives took over.

Nicholas' long message made my birthday. We began talking every day. Three months later, as Christmas approached, he asked me if I ever went back to Denver. We agreed to spend a couple of days skiing. Both of us, I'm sure, thinking this was a safe-ish way to see if there was a real spark between us. Five days into our date, that was it.

In February 2009, I flew to The Netherlands. Nicholas and I had a lovely reunion. I found a Master's program near where he lived and looked into transferring to The Agency's Amsterdam office. It would have been easier if I was a creative. For an American creative to get a visa, the company hiring them just has to prove they have a different creative vision than anyone in the EU—which is vague enough to be easy to do. If you're not a mighty creative, your company has to show you're better suited for a job than anyone in the EU.

But whatever happened, whatever it took, I was moving to Amsterdam to be with Nicholas. If that meant leaving The Agency, so be it.

I'd just gotten back from spending Valentine's weekend in Amsterdam with Nicholas when I was laid off. I was so jet-lagged and on a high when I arrived at The Agency on the Monday morning that I didn't realize what the invitation to the Cave meant.

I sat down on a poop-covered pebble and listened as the executive creative director told me The Agency was letting me go. It was like she was talking to me through a thick glass door. I may well have been smiling. The problem was I'd made a tactical error. A few weeks before, I'd been invited to transfer to the digital department. I said, "No Thanks" because I was focused on setting myself up in Amsterdam. What I didn't realize was that it wasn't an optional job transfer. I was expected to take the job. Or at least that was the reason The Agency gave for deciding to let me go. They gave me a decent severance but I was still pissed.

There's nothing worse than being dumped by someone just as you're getting ready to dump them.

———◆———

Still, at the party my friends at The Agency threw for me, I got to give the gracious goodbye speech I'd prepared months in advance. I invited Rita and, as I'd hoped, she and Brook liked each other. Towards the end of the party, at the bar near The Agency where I'd spent so much of the past three years, the three of us were sunk into a sofa, shoulder to shoulder, me in the middle.

"I always told her she was too nice for advertising," Brook said.

Rita giggled. "So did I!"

"Maybe I am," I said. "But I did my best."

"The trouble is, Liz, you were genetically programmed to have a brood of babies and make donuts. I blame Minnesota," Brook said.

"Nah," Rita said. "I think our Liz is going to do great things. I have no idea what but I'm sure she will."

"Thanks, Rita." I said. "That's the nicest thing you've ever said to me."

"It's because I know I'll never see you again," Rita laughed as I pretended to throw my drink in her face.

I thought about telling Rita and Brook about the woman from UNICEF I'd sat next to on one of my flights to the Netherlands. By the time we were over Nova Scotia, I'd decided to join UNICEF and spend my time saving the world. The problem was I needed a Master's. This was getting to be a bit of a recurring theme. I'd always wanted one, so that was fine with me.

Instead I raised my glass and shouted, "Odin's Beard!"

The whole bar went silent. Then, starting with Brook, one by one all my friends raised their glass, bottle or whatever they happened to be holding in the air, and cried "Odin's Beard!"

And I burst into tears.

———————

My yearning to help people by studying them and trying to figure out how to make their lives better came from the heart. Life at The Agency had been glamorous but it was really all about selling, or persuading if you want to be nice about it. Even though I was fascinated by psychology and research, I'd always felt my job was insubstantial to the point of being silly compared to what someone like Rita did. And I could care less about going to another fabulous party. Unless Prince was playing, of course.

But, although I'd realized that The Agency was an iron fist inside a velvet glove, I would always be thankful for what I'd learned. The Agency got the best out of people by intentionally pairing them with their opposites. The pathologically messy art director and the OCD writer would have no choice but to find a shared voice. And, although they'd fight tooth and nail and usually beg to be reassigned to someone they believed would be more simpatico, these opposites would end up loving the mismatch so much they'd spend years together.

I learned so much from this approach. This book is the product of working with someone who's quite different from me and it's been a fantastic experience.

Another thing I learned from The Agency was to never stay too late at Disneyland. Leave when the party's winding down but is still fun. It's sometimes brutal but it always works.

———◆———

I got my Masters and started on my PhD. A PhD has always represented the ultimate in academic freedom for me: you pick a subject that's all your own to explore but you must be able to map it in a way that stands up to the toughest criticism.

My professor Tibert Verhagen, PhD, who worked in the Business Department of the VU Amsterdam studying emerging technology and consumer behavior has become the mentor I've always wanted. Which made me realize that I'd been desperate for one all my life. It's probably why I gravitated towards Brook. Tibert helped me choose the subject for my PhD. But first a little backstory.

———◆———

I studied neurofeedback when I was in high school. This is basically the idea of modifying brainwaves to alter mental states, affecting many aspects of brain functioning including moods and things like concentration and memory. My interest in the subject really rose out of studying the consequences of brain injury after I was in car accident—the accident I didn't tell Nate about. A neuropsychologist who specialized in EEG Biofeedback and other strategies designed to affect brain functioning, helped me retrain my own brain. From then on, I had it at the back of my mind that I wanted to help people learn how to literally use their brains to take back control of their lives. But more about that later.

When I saw my first wearable back in 2006, at the store where I exchanged my New Balance running shoes for a pair by Escalate, I was fascinated. But I didn't know then that I was holding the missing piece of a puzzle in my hand.

Wearable technology offers us extraordinary insight into the way we behave and how to alter our behavior. It enables us to measure and monitor how we move, eat, drink and sleep. When we're armed with information about ourselves, we have the power to change our bodies and, through tools like mindfulness apps, our minds.

To me, it was obvious that wearables had enormous potential for proactive health care, for our bodies and minds. And the great thing was that in 2016 when I started my research in the Netherlands, other researchers were primarily working with the old and sick. I figured that the best way to test the empowering potential of wearables was to work with healthy, happy people in a country with a high quality of life where burnout was on the rise. I wanted to see how wearables could benefit healthy people with unhealthy habits and, specifically, if they could help beat burnout. This was the subject of my first research paper.

Researching into wearables led me to become interested in employee health. Which is how I came to get in touch with CBRE and meet Wouter.

Anticipating the research

My research project was funded by CBRE. I worked with the University of Twente, where I was a PhD student, as well as the publicly funded Vrije Universiteit (VU) Amsterdam. "Vrije Universiteit" translates as "Independent University." Given the subject of my research, I liked the association with independence.

When I first got in touch with Twente I wasn't a student at the university but I was studying at the VU. My first research paper considered ways in which wearable technology produced feelings of empowerment and led to a long-term commitment to achieving health goals. I needed a third reader for my first publication before it could go to the publisher. So, I approached a brilliant neuro-cognitive psychologist at Twente named Matthijs Noordzij, PhD.

Although the study of wearable technologies is new to many universities, it has been studied at Twente for over a decade. Matthijs's input into my paper was invaluable.

As my Healthy Offices project developed after I'd gotten the green light from Wouter at CBRE, I realized that, as usual, I'd taken on something hugely ambitious. My professor Tibert Verhagen and I believed that researching employee health included not just business, but medical, and psychological issues at the same time. We needed a bigger team than just the two of us. We approached Matthijs Noordzij about joining the team and also Miriam Vollenbroek, PhD, a tenured professor in the Biomedical Engineering Department. Miriam was the key to it all. She saw the potential of the project and spoke to the university. Twente accepted my application and I joined the Biosensors and Signals department under Miriam's guidance. I learned quickly why she was one of the youngest tenures at the University.

Before we began the research project in CBRE's offices I thought I should test my hypotheses by experimenting on myself. What I discovered would set the scene for my research findings. I found out that although I wasn't as bad as I'd been at The Agency I still had plenty of unhealthy work habits. I was shocked but this made me even more of a convert to the cause of creating healthy offices through technology.

Although my research project was set to run for seven months, the first two months involved me simply observing working life in CBRE's offices.

In those first two months my biggest challenge was not to trigger what's called the Hawthorne Effect. This is named after a series of experiments conducted at the Hawthorne, Chicago factory of Western Electric in the 1920's and 30's. The experiments, conducted by a sociologist named Elton Mayo, were originally set up to study the effects of physical conditions on productivity.

Mayo divided workers in the factory into two groups. One group had the lighting in its working area improved dramatically. For the other group, it stayed the same. The researchers were startled to discover that the workers in the brighter lit area became far more productive than the group whose lighting remained unchanged.

You would think that this had something to do with the effects of light on productivity and, as I'll show later, it does. But productivity also improved when other changes were made. When employees were given different working hours or more rest breaks, for instance. It actually improved when the lights in their area were dimmed again. Even after everything was returned to the way it was before, productivity remained higher than ever and absenteeism was at an all-time low. What was going on?

Before every change was made, Mayo told the workers that it was going to happen. After a while he realized it wasn't so much the physical changes themselves that made the difference but the simple fact that the workers felt someone cared about their working conditions. Mayo's research was groundbreaking because he established that the innate abilities of an employee were only part of the story. Individual performance is influenced by a person's surroundings and who they work with.

Mayo also discovered that discussing the changes before they were made prepared people to work differently. It's this phenomenon that gives the Hawthorne Effect its name. I didn't want people to know what my research was going to be about in advance, so although they knew it was going to happen, they didn't know what form it would take.

I worked on preparing my research and was politely evasive when people fished for clues about what I was doing. Meanwhile, I watched as people did what they do in so many offices—drink too much coffee, eat far too much sugar and salt, and work longer hours than they're contracted for at their mentally taxing jobs.

I found the way CBRE's employees worked kind of disturbing. I thought the Dutch had figured out the work-life balance thing.

In the Netherlands, this is considered a basic human right rather than a goal. The Netherlands is often rated among the top five countries in Europe for health and happiness. This is partly because of the attitude of the government, healthcare and an affordable standard of living but it's helped by employers themselves.

A common joke in the Netherlands is that if you call a business at 4:50 p.m. they may not answer in case the call takes more than ten minutes and they'll have to start working overtime. All jokes aside, this mentality has made the Dutch incredibly successful. Dutch businesses have a strong track record for being innovative, collaborative, and highly profitable. Over the last few years, however, the Dutch burnout rates had risen and employee sickness was on the rise[2]. If burnout could happen here, it could happen anywhere. Watching CBRE's employees at work, it was clear that this was the case. But why?

2   *http://publications.tno.nl/publication/34623350/pyzrBK/TNO-2016-working.pdf*

Creating an environment in which people are less likely to burn out or, in an ideal world, not burn out at all, is fundamental to my research and to the consultancy I have created with CBRE. The problem is that, although we all know burnout exists, we struggle to define it.

Identifying the broader business-cultural, social and even political reasons why burnout happens would be the territory of another research project and book entirely. But it is possible to study the conditions that have the potential to cause burnout within a specific office environment, which is what we did.

Before we go any further, I'd like to offer a brief history and working definition of the term "burnout" for the purposes of this book.

American psychologist Herbert Freudenberger came up with the term "burnout" in the 1970's. He first applied it to "helping" professions in the US like medicine—to doctors and nurses, for example. Later in the 1970's, Japanese people began dying from overwork in frightening numbers, which helped raise the profile of burnout dramatically.

The Japanese didn't have a name for burnout so they came up with karóshi, which means "overwork death" and describes occupational sudden mortality. The main causes are heart attack and stroke due to stress and a starvation diet. Suicide is also included as a cause of death from karóshi.

A Japanese government report published in 2016 estimated that one in five Japanese workers was at risk of death from overwork. This is the first report the government has published on karóshi. While it's heartening that the Japanese government has admitted to the scale of the problem, it's a little unnerving to think that it's taken 40 years.

The extreme nature of karóshi has also perhaps served to minimize the danger of burnout in other countries. Also, because the effects of burnout are not likely to be as dramatic as karóshi, it's hard to point to symptoms that are as clear cut as a heart attack or stroke. It's especially difficult because, while we can identify the physical and mental manifestations of poor health, there is no fixed idea of what health actually is.

In 1948, the World Health Organization (WHO) defined health as "a state of complete physical, mental, and social well-being and not merely the absence of disease or infirmity." The definition was revised in 1984 to become "the extent to which an individual or group is able to realize aspirations and satisfy needs, and to change or cope with the environment. Health is a resource for everyday life, not the objective of living; it is a positive concept, emphasizing social and personal resources, as well as physical capacities."[3]

While the redefinition was done to make health more measurable, when you stop and think about it, this shift in definition by the WHO is rather sad. We've gone from believing that a state of "complete, physical, mental and social well-being" is possible to

3   *https://en.wikipedia.org/wiki/Health (Accessed June 18, 2017)*

defining it as simply the capability to "change or cope with the environment." There's a story here, for another time.

The 1984 definition has enormous implications for employee and organizational health. If you make health a "positive concept" it becomes a resource. Healthy employees are an asset so it makes sense for an organization to do everything it can to safeguard and encourage their health. This also brings into play the question of personal responsibility within an organizational environment.

When I was at The Agency, no one ever told me not to stay late to the point that more than once I was still at my desk when the sun came up. Don't forget that I was 23 and this was my first experience of working in a truly creative, high-powered environment. I was desperate to prove myself. And I had the example of people many years older than me who'd been trained to succeed in the ultra-competitive world of corporate America. A world that is unlikely to change until managers step up and offer real leadership and guidance in how to work in a healthy way.

Without guidance, how is any young person entering the world of work meant to find the sweet spot at which they're working hard enough to do their job to the best of their ability and feel fulfilled but not to the extent that they're ruining their health?

It's especially hard because, as with the state of health itself, there's no universal consensus as to the definition of burnout. It's not recognized as a distinct disorder in the Diagnostic and Statistical Manual of Mental Disorders. It is included in the International Statistical Classification of Diseases and Related Health Problems but not as a disorder. You'll find it under problems related to life-management difficulty.

There have been attempts to measure burnout and separate it from other illnesses. Questionnaires have been created for this purpose but they're generally regarded as not particularly accurate. The Maslach Burnout Inventory (MBI)[4] for instance was developed as a research tool and not a method of diagnosis. Right now, many experts agree on three signs of burnout. People feel constantly physically and emotionally exhausted. They feel alienated and find their jobs more and more stressful and frustrating. Performance at work suffers because people with burnout find it hard to concentrate.

These are essentially symptoms of depression, which is acknowledged as a "real" condition. One of the ways to separate burnout from depression, and avoid giving people treatment and medication that might be harmful for them, is to try and establish whether work is the only thing in their lives that makes them feel exhausted, stressed and unable to concentrate. Which is easier said than done.

Countries themselves don't agree on a definition of burnout. In countries such as the Netherlands or Sweden, employees who believe they're burning out are sent to a doctor for diagnosis. They can receive a pre-burnout warning or be diagnosed with full burnout. In both cases, the doctor is obliged to advise the person's employer on how to change their work duties to avoid burnout. If the employee is already burned out, the doctor will order the employer to put them immediately on bed rest for a certain time frame depending on the diagnosis.

Burnout then is something that can be defined and diagnosed but only if you live in the right country.

The problem is of course that, as with any health problem, it's up to an employee to go to a doctor if they believe they're

---

4   Maslach, C., & Jackson, S. E. (1981). *"The measurement of experienced burnout."* Journal of organizational behavior, 2(2), 99-113.

suffering from burnout. When I burned out at The Agency, I knew I was feeling mentally and physically unwell but I thought it went with the territory. I lived with low-level—and then not so low—poor health but I couldn't point to a single cause like a virus, for instance. So, like everyone at The Agency, I soldiered on. Because that was "rock and roll." The show must go on and you're weak if you complain.

That also meant not taking perfectly justified sick days and self-medicating with medicines like Dayquil. It's apparently not unusual for people who give burnout as the reason they're quitting their jobs to have unused sick or vacation days. That may strike you as bizarre because you'd think you would grab any chance you could to take a day off if you felt sick or exhausted all the time. But remember that I burned out at The Agency and I didn't use any sick days.

Comparing the corporate, organizational world with rock and roll is highly dangerous in my opinion. We all know the horror stories about the Amy Winehouses and Kurt Cobains of rock and roll: seriously damaged addicts who were indulged rather than helped because they were so incredibly talented. On a far lesser, or at least much less romantic scale, life at The Agency was fueled too much by stimulants, from coffee to Adderall.

More recently, I've read reports of people in Silicon Valley microdosing on psychedelics like LSD because they believe it enhances their creativity. It probably does but miscalculating the amount of LSD you dose yourself with can be highly dangerous and for some people there's no coming back. I find it disturbing that young people are playing with their mental health simply to be better at work.

There's also the idea that any kind of setback can be overcome by willpower. And what better example of willpower is there than ambition or drive? We all admire ambitious, driven people who don't give up. They're the ones who do the outstanding work and show the levels of dedication that organizations thrive on. I wanted, and want, to be one of those people.

But we pay a price for being ambitious. As my mother told me when I was starry-eyed about working at The Agency. The price of ignoring signs of physical and mental ill health caused by overwork is that we collapse precisely when we can't afford to.

If we ambitious people are potentially our own worst enemies, what are employers supposed to do? Is it their responsibility when a valuable employee is heading in the direction of burnout? I would say yes for ethical reasons but, more to the point, because it makes sound business sense. When your biggest investment is in people, it seems utterly crazy to let them burn out.

This is why the healthy office consultancy we've created with CBRE emphasizes the bottom line. The changes to the office environment I'm about to describe will only be superficial unless they're the manifestation of a profound change in the way an organization regards and treats its people.

Creating healthier office environments is not just about saving money. It's an investment in the future. A healthy office will attract the right kind of employees, the "radical workers" organizations are so keen to attract in order to stay out in front and adapt to the future of work. It will add enormous value and the cost of transformation is far less than you think.

My professor and I agreed that my multidisciplinary study would examine the environmental effects of the workplace on employee health. It would involve the departments of Neurocognitive Psychology, Biomedical Engineering at the University of Twente and the Business department at the VU.

A belief that environments have the potential to change our behavior is fundamental to my research. As Elton Mayo's research showed all those years ago, the physical aspect of a working environment has a huge influence on the way people behave. But although working conditions have improved enormously since what you might call modern offices appeared in the 18th century, they still have a long way to go.

Our project measured the effect of environmental and healthy lifestyle changes on 124 people in the CBRE Amsterdam office over seven months. The study used surveys, experiments, biological data, movement tracking, daily ratings, and interviews.

After reviewing the literature on the subject, we selected five changes in the working environment that would in theory have the most impact on employee health and potential. Each month we chose one change to implement to see how it individually would affect the employees' work. The next month we would remove the change and implement the next one.

We divided the changes into environmental adjustments and healthy choices. The environmental adjustments related to natural space and lighting. People taking part in the project didn't have a choice over whether they were in the adjusted environment or not.

The three healthy choices were optional. They were healthy nutrition, mental balance, and physical exercise.

To establish a baseline, we observed and collected data for two months before changing anything in the environment. After this, we created a healthy spot in the office where we made all the changes.

The 124 people taking part in the research were divided into three groups. Group one sat in the healthy spot and wore activity trackers that monitored their health data and provided feedback to help them improve their activity and sleep. The technology also included gamified elements to inspire motivation and daily progress. Gamification is using elements of game playing such as point scoring or competing with others to encourage engagement with devices or services. In healthcare, it's used to engage patients and improve their health. Using gamification techniques provided feedback, and encouraged participants to meet goals and compete against friends and family. Group Two also sat in the healthy spot but didn't wear the activity trackers. This allowed us to see to what extent activity trackers influenced the behavior of Group One. Group Three was a control group and experienced no changes. The difference between them and Group One and Two allowed us to measure the effect of sitting in the healthy spot as well as the influence of the technology.

The research:
what we did

Technology was an integral part of the entire project. For our study, we used beacons to measure movement and space usage in the office as well as wearable technology wristbands for the participants, to encourage healthy sleep and activity.

What we did

At the start of the research we gave the CBRE employees who were going to be monitored by wearables the option to choose two daily goals. They could either set their goal at the recommended 10,000 steps every day—the equivalent of walking or running around five miles (eight kilometers)—or choose a different step amount. The second goal was based on hours of sleep, including both deep (REM) and lighter sleep. Many people set their goal at around eight hours of sleep a night, which is what the device recommended.

The beacons we used detected movement in people wearing the wristbands and identified patterns of activity and traffic flow in areas where they were activated. We used the beacons not just to monitor employee movement but to analyze how space was used with a view to optimizing it in the future.

The research: healthy nutrition

In the office environment, healthy nutrition begins with tackling coffee and sugar. Followed by healthy eating and drinking in general.

Today, more than ever, drinking coffee is an integral part of office life. The emergence of coffee shops like Starbucks since the 1990's, with their emphasis on the hip, gourmet aspect of coffee drinking, has made a major contribution to its popularity. The quality of the coffee consumed in offices has improved immeasurably, making it more appealing. But potentially more dangerous.

Medical professionals advise a maximum of five cups of coffee a day, which is the equivalent of 400 milligrams of caffeine. According to the US Food & Drug Administration, this amount of caffeine a day is safe for healthy adults who aren't pregnant or sensitive to caffeine. It does, however, increase circulating cortisol (the stress hormone) concentrations. Higher cortisol levels are associated with rapid weight gain, high blood pressure, muscle weakness, mood swings, anxiety and depression, impaired cognitive functioning (fuzzy brain), and poor sleep, among other things. After drinking a cup of coffee, cortisol concentrations are significantly higher.[5] And this effect lasts for approximately 60 minutes.

Before I started my research, I monitored my own habits and was surprised at how much coffee I drank every day, usually stemming from the belief that it would give me energy. Those

5   Gavrieli, A., Yannakoulia, M., Fragopoulou, E., Margaritopoulos, D., Chamberland, J. P., Kaisari, P., Kavouras, S. & Mantzoros, C. S. (2011). *"Caffeinated coffee does not acutely affect energy intake, appetite, or inflammation but prevents serum cortisol concentrations from falling in healthy men."* The Journal of nutrition, 141(4), 703-707.

of us who believe we need coffee to get us going in the morning or wake ourselves up later in the day are raising our levels of cortisol, the stress hormone, at the same time. Being stressed doesn't help our decision-making. Drinking coffee in the afternoon or evening can also disrupt our sleep.

Sugar is another staple of office consumption. Office reception areas often have chocolate, mints, or jelly candies set out in bowls. From one perspective, this makes sense. The organization a person is visiting appears generous and welcoming.

Eating sugar causes your dopamine levels to spike. Dopamine is a neurotransmitter that is released when dopamine neurons are activated. It influences our desire for pleasure and is released by naturally rewarding experiences such as food, sex, and abuse of drugs. Most of the drugs we abuse cause dopamine to be released, which is one of the reasons they're addictive. The more we use them, the more we want them.

One of the most surprising and alarming things I came across in my research was a brain scan showing that sugar activates almost exactly the same part of the brain as cocaine does.

Without being too sensationalist, it's generally agreed that a person high on cocaine is capable of making pretty dumb decisions and that the high is often followed by a low that makes the person anxious and irritable. Discovering that sugar does essentially the same thing but in a milder way is pretty unnerving.

Sugar consumption has risen by 50% since 1970. When we consume sugar our dopamine levels rise, making us feel good. Some of us become addicted. Apart from the obvious damage sugar addiction does to our physical health in the form of obesity and Type 2 diabetes, sugar compromises nerve cells' ability to communicate, making it harder to remember instructions, process ideas and handle our emotions. It's not surprising then that many doctors are advocating making sugar a restricted substance, like alcohol or cigarettes. Governments are also attempting to introduce legislation that restricts the amount of sugar in our food and drinks.

But this is a long way from becoming a reality and, in any case, people who are addicted to caffeine and sugar have built up the habit over many years. As anyone who has gone on a coffee detox knows, withdrawing from coffee is unpleasant. Caffeine withdrawal symptoms include headaches, fatigue and drowsiness, depressed mood and irritability, difficulty concentrating, and a variety of flu-like symptoms. Headaches can be intense and last for 21 days.

What we did

Although we didn't remove coffee altogether we did remove carbonated sodas during the month we studied/changed nutrition at the office. We attempted to limit coffee drinking, especially in the afternoon, by setting out pitchers of water filled with mint, cucumber and various fruits. These colorful pitchers blocked the view of the grey coffee machine and were the first thing people saw entering the eating area. The amount of decaffeinated tea on offer was increased to 30%.

Why didn't we remove coffee altogether? Because it wasn't realistic. Caffeine is addictive and had it not been provided in the workspace, employees would likely have frequented local coffee shops or brought their own. Reducing caffeine consumption to a healthy level was enough.

I have to say I didn't give the question of the effect of drinking carbonated sodas as much thought as I should have. I quit drinking them a couple of years ago and had forgotten how stimulating and reviving all those bubbles can be. Bubbles excite our taste receptors and and can make drinks seem more interesting when we drink them.

I once saw a study where people's brains were scanned as they were shown pictures of Coca-Cola. They lit up like Christmas trees. I always thought that this was in anticipation of receiving that hit of caffeine and sugar but it could just as easily be because of the physically pleasurable associations.

Before the study, CBRE offers employees liter bottles of cola that employees can drink by the glass. These glasses are fairly small—around a third to a quarter of the size of a normal can of soda. The intention was good. Smaller glasses should reduce consumption but in this case, it caused the reverse reaction. People would bring a whole bottle of cola back to their desks and drink it throughout the day even though they wouldn't dream of guzzling three cans of soda. This could be explained by the Delboeuf illusion[6] where people misjudge the size of circles depending on the amount of empty space around them. Food scientists and nutritionists argue that bigger plates make portions look smaller than they are. Glasses are smaller than bottles so people think they're drinking less.

We also provided healthy snacks like nuts, avocados, and very dark chocolate every afternoon an hour or two after lunch, when people often experience sugar cravings. These snacks were extremely popular, even with people who weren't taking part in the research. When the nutrition month was finished and we stopped providing the snacks, we received complaints. This also happened when CBRE stopped providing free soda.

6   *https://en.wikipedia.org/wiki/Delboeuf_illusion (Accessed 18 June, 2017)*

The research: mental balance

There is no question that mindfulness and yoga are incredibly empowering tools for relaxation, improving a person's mood and overall mental state. To give just a couple of examples, a study done by John Hopkins University[7] showed that mindfulness meditation reduces symptoms of depression, anxiety, and pain, equal to or greater than the effect of an antidepressant. According to Yale University, mindfulness meditation positively affects the Default Mode Network connectivity in the brain, enabling meditators to focus more effectively[8].

Studies have also shown that practicing mindfulness, meditation and yoga enhances a person's ability to empathize.

Mindfulness is becoming increasingly popular in the workplace with spaces being set aside for mindfulness and yoga. This probably has something to do with the influence of Silicon Valley on work culture. Silicon Valley has not only developed the start-up culture but also adopted every form of mindfulness, meditation, and yoga. Mindfulness is the mental state achieved by focusing on the present moment while accepting our thoughts, emotions and feelings without judgment. Mindfulness and meditation have been used to combat burnout in the workplace.

However, the problem with teaching employees to meditate without changing a pressure-filled environment is that it puts the responsibility on them. In the extreme work environments of many American or start-up companies, this ends up being

7   http://www.hopkinsmedicine.org/news/media/releases/meditation_for_anxiety_and_de-pression (Accessed 18 June, 2017)

8   Bill Hathaway, "Tuning out: how brains benefit from meditation" (November 21, 2011) http://news.yale.edu/2011/11/21/tuning-out-how-brains-benefit-meditation (Accessed 18 June, 2017)

like meditating in a house on fire. It will calm employees down for a bit but won't stop them from going up in flames.

As with every part of the research, I experimented on myself first. I enjoy meditation but struggle with getting into the right headspace, especially when I'm stressed. I wondered if CBRE's employees would face the same problem and whether they'd be able to practice in the office.

What we did

For the month in which we focused on mindfulness and meditation, we set aside two rooms for meditation—guided, as well as a combination of relaxing sound and images—yoga, naps and weekly massages. Five, 10 and 15-minute yoga sessions took place in a private conference room. Weekly chair massages lasted for 15 minutes each. Although we made people aware that these existed, we didn't push them. Our aim was to see if people chose these practices themselves and, if so, what happened.

In order to allow a more concentrated and relaxing work environment people could also choose to wear noise cancelling headphones in the main office to block out distracting noise.

We conducted a stress test experiment to test the effects of mindfulness on employees. This was a simple test in four different environments. Two were stress inducing and two were in rooms adapted to be conducive to mindfulness. In each environment people had to complete an accuracy test where they would strike through all of one type of letter over the course of ten minutes. The letter "A" for example. They were then rotated between a stressful environment and a mindful or meditative one equally, decreasing the potential effect of a learning curve.

In one of the stressful environments we asked people to say why they were better at their job than their colleagues. This kind of thing is reasonably common in the US but it makes Europeans uncomfortable and increases their stress level. The employees were 30% less accurate in the stressful environment than in the meditative one. We asked people to complete a questionnaire to rate their stress levels in the different environments and, unsurprisingly, they rated the stressful environments as high stress and the meditative as low stress.

When we took people into the second stressful environment and asked them to speak in public—at the top of the list of people's biggest fears—they performed 16% worse than in the meditative environment.[9]

The research: physical exercise

In 2014, The Huffington Post sensationally christened sitting the new smoking. While it's perhaps not as dangerous as that, we all know that keeping active is good for our health. It produces the good cholesterol that reduces the unhealthy triglycerides that help cause heart disease, for instance. Research also indicates that physical activity increases the circulation of "feel-good" hormones like serotonin, helping them make their way to receptors, suggesting that being active can alleviate and prevent the symptoms of depression.

According to a survey of 9,000 women published in the American Journal of Preventative Medicine, those who sat for more than seven hours a day were 47% more likely to be depressed than women who sat for four hours or less. Women

9   Glenn Croston, PhD, "The Thing we Fear More Than Death", (November 29, 2012) https:// www.psychologytoday.com/blog/the-real-story-risk/201211/the-thing-we-fear-more-death

who never exercised had a 99% higher risk of developing depression than those who exercised at least minimally.[10]

Sitting for long periods of time has also been shown to affect blood sugar and insulin levels. Research done by Henson et al., (2013) analyzed the outcomes of 18 studies spanning almost 800,000 people and concluded that individuals who moved less were twice as likely to develop type 2 diabetes. A study by Patel et al. (2010) found that men and women who sat for longer than six hours a day died sooner than those who sat for three or less.

It's not surprising then that some doctors recommend standing up as much as 32 times every work day or at least twice every hour (Storrs, 2015). Which is all very well and good but employees in an office are expected to be at their desks, hard at work and accountable for large parts of the day. So how does an employee stay active and what can organizations do to help?

What we did

We realized that it wasn't possible to encourage people to jump up and down four times an hour so we provided healthy alternatives to sitting on chairs. CBRE is a property management company that works very much like most consultancy agencies. They work on billable hours, have lots of set meetings and employees usually spend an hour or two in the car every day. It's also a formal work environment, which means suits and nice shoes but no workout clothes or Nike shoes. Providing these people with an environment that helped them be more active was going to be a challenge.

---

10   Van Uffelen, J. G., van Gellecum, Y. R., Burton, N. W., Peeters, G., Heesch, K. C., & Brown, W. J. (2013). "Sitting-time, physical activity, and depressive symptoms in mid-aged women." American journal of preventive medicine, 45(3), 276-281.

People in groups One and Two were offered medicine balls, stationary bicycles, and treadmills connected to desks. In one of the conference rooms we replaced a regular table with a counter height conference table where people could stand while they worked and also provided chairs with pedals.

To increase movement when people were sitting and improve balance and strength when they were standing, we introduced yoga balls, active stools (a mushroom shaped balancing seat), and balancing boards.

Wherever possible we promoted the idea of walking at lunchtime and having walking meetings. We made a map that showed paths near the office that were ideal for walking meetings and showed the estimated time for each walk. This also introduced fresh air and natural sunlight into the employee's day.

The research: healthy lighting

We don't think about it all that much but decades of research have shown that light can substantially influence our mood and ability to focus. It really all comes down to what are called our circadian rhythms. These are physical, mental and behavioral changes over a roughly 24-hour cycle as a response to light and darkness.

Apparently, this is because we have evolved under conditions that we find in Central Africa, where there is on average 12 hours of daylight and 12 hours of night. It's why people in southern European countries, where there's more sunlight, are less likely to suffer from depression than those in northern Europe.

Whatever we do to change lighting, people will always have different rhythms. This is partly due to genetics. Some people are what's called early chronotypes, which means they wake up early and full of energy and want to fall asleep early too.

Others are late chronotypes who find it hard to get going in the morning and come alive later at night.

Which is why the whole notion of working from nine to five will result in greater productivity for some employees and be problematic for others.

Circadian rhythms affect when we wake up and go to sleep as well as our energy levels and moods throughout the day. When these schedules are out of sync, we can become euphoric, manic or less alert, vigilant and attentive. Any of these conditions can affect executive functions of our brain. Executive functions include those cognitive processes necessary to select and monitor behaviors that enable us to achieve certain goals. These include planning ability and being able to anticipate the consequences of our actions. For example, being aware that we shouldn't swear in a job interview.

If circadian rhythms are interrupted or disturbed, it can change a person's work habits. Changes can include staying at the office longer, throwing them out of their circadian rhythm for the days and nights that follow.

I knew that my research at CBRE had to involve light but I wasn't sure precisely where to start. I started working with the team at German lighting manufacturer Osram. They jumped at the opportunity to help me with my research because I was the first person they'd come across who was studying lighting in offices as part of an integrated study of employees and the environment in which they work.

This is important for people like Osram because they need to convince organizations of the value of human centric lighting in a typical office space.

The team helped me understand why lighting in offices must address real human needs. It's all about getting as close to natural light within an office environment as possible. But they also made it very clear that lighting had to be part of an entire office environment revolution.

Before we started the research project, I experimented on myself. The first day after I changed the lighting in my home office I went in to send an email and emerged seven hours later having completed lots of work. The problem was that I was buzzing from a "light high" and it took me hours to come down. I realized that experimenting with lighting in the office would be as much about finding a way for people to unwind in the evening as it would be about stimulating them to be more productive.

What we did

The lighting environment at CBRE was normal for most office environments. But the Osram team told me it needed to change dramatically. Apparently, it was perfect for people who were relaxing after work or getting ready for bed. This was a revelation for two reasons.

First of all, the lighting at CBRE was the opposite of what it should be in terms of employee productivity. Secondly, it was typical for offices. Which meant that most offices are lit in a way that is unhelpful to the people working in them. We realized we had to completely redesign the lighting in the office.

To help people develop healthy sleep patterns and energy levels, we installed a lighting timer on a circadian-friendly schedule in the place we'd designated as the healthy spot and almost doubled the brightness of the lighting. Lighting was warm in the morning, very strong and bright in the early afternoon and dimmer in the late afternoon.

We mostly directed light sources at the wall to mimic the sensation of daylight coming in through a window and to avoid glare. But in some places we lowered lighting sources from the ceiling to allow light to bathe the correct part of a person's face—reaching the photoreceptors in the eye that influence circadian rhythms.

Lighting changed from a yellow tint to a blue one in the afternoon but returned to a softer yellow light towards the end of the day.

The research: nature in offices

Most of us have experienced a feeling of tranquility and relaxation sitting on a beach listening to the waves. It's also believed that green spaces like gardens and parks promote serenity and wellbeing. In recent years, research has attempted to measure and identify the beneficial effects of natural spaces. Medical research into the possible effects of plants on patient outcomes has suggested that people recover faster in environments with plants than those without. It seems that plants can also help to prevent and remedy headaches, depression, anxiety disorders, asthma, heart disease, and physiological stress. They help with concentration and self-discipline. The interesting thing is that changes can happen in a matter of hours or minutes rather than as a result of long-term exposure.[11]

Evidence suggests that these benefits can even come from fake plants, posters, or wall murals.

Today, most offices have some sort of plant life. But plants are usually spread out pretty randomly and density usually adds

11   Ulrich, R, *Paper for conference* (2002). *"Plants for People, Health Benefits of Gardens in Hospitals."*

up to 1% of what it would be in an outside, naturally green area. This despite the fact that studies like one involving 3,600 workers in eight countries in Europe, Middle East and Africa (EMEA) show that employees who work in environments with natural elements have a 13% higher level of well-being and are 8% more productive. [12]

What we did

Before we started, the only greenery in the CBRE offices was artificial. Potted flowers were placed near coffee areas and very few of them were visible from work spaces.

We distributed real and fake plants in the healthy areas, in the centers of work spaces and in eating areas, and put murals of trees and forests on walls. Once we'd done this, every workspace in the healthy area had a view of a plant—real, fake, or pictured in a mural.

After the dust had settled

When I'm in the middle of a research project, I'm focused on the details and making sure I'm gathering as much accurate data as possible. This was the biggest and longest research project I'd ever conducted so I worked extremely hard at keeping the technology functioning and making sure the monthly changes happened smoothly.

12   Karen Higginbottom, "Employees Working In Offices With Natural Elements Report Higher Well Being", https://www.forbes.com/sites/karenhigginbottom/2014/10/21/employees-working-in-offices-with-natural-elements-report-higher-well-being/#ea3b22262e1d

Wouter was closely involved and we met at least once a week. Like everyone else at CBRE, he was kept in the dark as to how the project was going. Still, he was patient and fought off the senior executives who wanted to know what the company was getting out of its investment in healthy food, new plants, massages and so on. Wouter was a great champion. He kept everyone away from me and let me get on with the research.

Because we were doing just about every type of research there is—surveys, daily responses, interviews, experiments and analyzing biological data—the support from my university was critical. It felt good to be backed up by a strong, diverse and thoughtful team.

Working with a team that understood the implications of my research was extremely important when it came to the data we were gathering. This was incredibly sensitive and personal. If it had been made available to CBRE, it could potentially lead to people being discriminated against. For example, if a manager sees that their employee isn't sleeping much and is feeling stressed or not as motivated they may pass them up for a promotion. However, that person might be working extra hard and not sleeping because they have a big project and are running on fumes.

Although I went into the project believing that sensitive personal data should not be owned by anyone, I hadn't realized what this really meant. I now understand why it's so valuable.

This is why the data we collected, as well as that gathered by the consultancy set up together with CBRE, should be owned by the university. Names and any distinguishing characteristics will be removed, leaving only data that any scientist researching employee health and healthcare in general is sure to find enormously helpful.

Clients of the service will receive comprehensive and insightful reports about the outcome of the study but results will be about the general population not individuals.

As my own results came in, it became clear that the changes we'd made really did make people feel healthier and happier. To be honest, I would have been surprised if this hadn't been the case. There were still some surprises along the way, though.

I'd assumed that not giving participants any clue as to what was coming next, nor informing them when the research would finish, would make them uncomfortable. For many the reverse was true. They enjoyed the idea that there was something new around the corner and were disappointed when the project ended. This says something about how beneficial it can be to introduce an element of healthy change into an office environment.

I have to say I didn't expect the huge backlash when we took the soda away. I'd forgotten how addictive soda can be. When I worked at The Agency we had a soda account and a free vending machine was installed. This had been one of my childhood fantasies and I had at least one free soda a day. Looking back, I was certainly addicted to the soda, as well as the idea that I was getting something for nothing. I'd weaned myself off soda so it didn't occur to me that people would have such strong reactions when their free soda vanished. To me, it was simply about removing a source of caffeine and sugar.

Months after ending the study, people were still complaining and I realized that the free soda was as much a reward, or perk, as it was an unhealthy habit. Removing the soda said something about CBRE's attitude towards its employees so we should probably have permanently replaced it with something that appeared equally appealing but was also healthy.

The research results

Our research goal was to see if it was possible to create an office ecosystem that used healthy environments, healthy choices, and technology, to optimize an employee's performance. We analyzed the interviews, surveys, daily responses, biological data and experiments through a variety of statistical tools to see the effect of environments on people's perceptions (i.e.: surveys, daily responses and interviews) performance (experiments) and health (biological data).

For each of the 5 months we conducted an experiment based on the methodology of an experiment conducted by Dr Roland Pepermans of the Vrije Universititeit Brussels. Sadly this project was never published but the methodology is found in other studies.

The strength of this methodology really lies in the rotation of the same people between different environments. Once in a new environment they are asked to complete a simple accuracy test. In our project, all participants received a few sheets of paper and were instructed to find and cross out all instances of one letter before moving on to the next page—for example the letter "V." Participants were given on average 10 minutes to finish the task before rotating to the next station. In total, there were four stations: two healthy and two unchanged.

Participants were rotated equally between healthy and unchanged, mitigating the risk of a learning curve on certain stations. It's important to note that we did not rotate people during the food experiment but simply tested them one time, once the food was in their bloodstream.

Change	Environmental adjustment or healthy choice	Improvement in task performance
Natural Space	Plants versus no plants	10%
Healthy Nutrition	Avocado and spinach smoothie versus Moorkop (cream filled donut). This experiment was conducted 25 minutes after drinking/eating.	45%
Healthy Lighting	Improved lighting versus old lighting	12%
Mental Balance	Mindfulness meditation versus stress-test	30%
Physical Exercise	Activity versus no activity 5-10 minutes on stationary bike seat until they feel their heart rate is elevated, but they were not hot or sweating.	12%

TECHNOLOGY

Introducing wearables had a profound effect on employee behavior. This was due to the targets employees chose, for example 10,000 steps and eight hours of sleep per day, and their changing attitude towards their health.

Employees started to relate to each other face to face more. For example, they would walk to each other's desks for an update, rather than send an email. This, of course, was because they needed to reach their step goal but it also arguably enriched and strengthened office relationships.

> **"I catch myself pressing the button and I walk to someone's desk instead of emailing them or chatting them, it's 50 steps"**
>
> —*Participant, healthy offices study*

Feedback from activity trackers didn't just affect employee behavior inside the office. Employees might choose to avoid an instant caffeine or sugar hit because they knew this would make it harder to sleep later. Instead, they would energize themselves by taking a walk in the afternoon.

Looking forward

When we collected the wearable devices at the end of the project, most employees told us they'd purchased a replacement or were looking for one. The benefits for organizations of inviting employees to wear devices are also clear, especially when gamification elements such as setting daily goals are introduced. Measuring activity using wearable technology would enable employers to set up office spaces in a way that encourages movement.

Although we used beacons in our research, we didn't enable them to send notifications to employee smartphones. However, the potential advantages of doing so are considerable. These notifications could be standard responses to different situations. For example, employees could get a notification on their phone to take the stairs when they're standing by the elevator. Responses could also be customized to the individual's behavior. These "just-in-time" customized notifications could sync with the health data on a phone or wearable device. For example, if a device shows that an individual didn't sleep well the night before, a customized notification may offer to reserve a desk or conference room with lots of light.

The benefits of wearable technology linked to smarter office systems are obvious to a scientist like myself or to an enlightened organization. Individual analytics and feedback can help employees understand their own bodies and minds, enabling them to work in a smarter, healthier way regardless of time or location. There are, however, employee rights to consider.

We are already seeing instances of organizations using technology to limit employee freedoms and to actually make working conditions worse. For example, one organization has been harshly criticized for tracking employee movement using GPS data to make sure people are working at a pace the employer has decided on.

Privacy laws are a hot topic when it comes to employee health and behavioral data and for good reason. Many security breaches have made businesses and employees wary of technology that collects their personal data. Laws on privacy and security vary greatly depending on the country. While the US has relatively flexible laws on employee data, The Netherlands has taken the opposite approach and put incredibly strict restrictions on health or personal data being gathered on employees.

The reason we were able to conduct this study is because the data was collected and managed by the University of Twente. During our study, other employee health studies that were conducted internally by other companies had to stop because of increased regulations. CBRE was never given access to the raw data, only some of the research results. Participants' data was anonymized and generalized to avoid any possibility of identifying and/or discriminating against an employee.

Ultimately, then, the presence of technology in offices must be shaped by an organization's own ethics backed up by robust legislation to protect employee privacy and rights in general.

How businesses implement their smart offices and what they do with the data is crucial. Many dynamics can either empower or suppress performance within an organization. Careful and humane decisions over data hoarding and privacy invasion will make the difference between success and counterproductive suspicion on the part of employees.

A clearly defined and ethical data-collection goal, transparent collection techniques and a commitment to prioritizing employee rights above all else are fundamental to creating a smart, healthy ecosystem at work.

HEALTHY NUTRITION

During our monthly survey, we consistently asked employees about their choices regarding beverages. These included water, caffeinated tea, and coffee.

The healthy snacks we provided each afternoon to try to maintain employees' energy levels and prevent them from crashing and reverting to unhealthy snacking were a big hit. After the nutrition month was over and the snacks were removed, people complained. They were one of the first things people asked to be returned once the research was over. The pitchers of water were also a big hit and something that was quickly brought back after the research had been completed.

The participants involved in the healthy implementations decreased their coffee intake by 47% and increased their water consumption. The healthy group went from 60% of people drinking the doctor recommended amount of coffee (< five cups per day) to 94%. This pattern continued into the next month, after the nutritional initiatives were taken away. More than 90% of the (healthy office) participants continued to drink less than five cups of coffee per day the following month.

THE STATS

45%   improvement of measured performance

14%   in self rated performance

78%   felt more energetic

66%   felt happier

63%   felt more alert

63%   drank more water

54%   were more aware of healthy ingredients/ foods

52%   felt more motivated

52%   felt healthier

51%   skipped unhealthy snacks they previously would have taken

32%   drank less coffee

Looking forward

The problem that remains is an office culture that almost worships coffee and relies on sweet things to not only energize but also act as comfort food.

To change employee behavior, organizations must influence nutrition in the office environment in a way that doesn't seem oppressive. More than one person told me that they found the pitchers of fruit and vegetable filled water to be pretty. We placed the colorful green, yellow, orange and red pitchers in front of the boring grey coffee machine. Given that one of the main aims in changing peoples' habits to make them healthier is drinking more water, it's amazing that water is not made more appealing.

As far as coffee is concerned, it's important to remember that the rise in its consumption is very much a result of increased availability and intense marketing. But coffee is a drug of sorts, because it causes a chemical reaction in our brains and bodies. Coffee is addictive. Persuading people to quit caffeine or reduce their consumption can be a slow and difficult task. Stopping abruptly, as anyone who's done a detox knows, can result in headaches and other painful symptoms. So how can we persuade people to go through a process they know to be uncomfortable?

Gamification—rewarding people who meet their set goals and celebrating these achievements as they reduce their consumption—combined with educating people as to how to stop as painlessly as possible could be the answer.

MENTAL BALANCE

Based on their experience during the research period, 68% of people who took part believed that they should have the opportunity to receive massage at work. The percentage of people who believed meditation should be available in the office was 32% and 29% believed yoga should be offered.

Although 23% believed a nap room was a good idea, several participants thought it would be hard to manage in practice and not something management would support.

Massages were fully booked from the first week of the research project but only by women. Men told us that they weren't so keen on the idea. But after hearing positive feedback from the women, a few men decided to try a massage. After these men spread the word about how much they'd enjoyed the experience, the mix of men and women having massages became equal.

Whether people meditated, practiced yoga or took a nap seemed to depend more on personal preference and if they thought these had a place in company culture.

"I really wanted to try out the nap room, but it didn't feel right to stop working for 20 minutes and go sleep. Maybe the nap room is a step too fast. The other experiences were excellent!"

—*Participant, healthy offices research*

THE STATS

30%   improvement of measured performance

14%   improvement of self rated performance

66%   felt more energized

63%   felt happier

56%   felt more motivated

53%   felt healthier

51%   felt more creative

Looking forward

Introducing mindfulness and yoga offered the clearest possible indicator of how altering an organization's culture can change individual employee behavior. I received more responses during the month focused on mindfulness than any other time from people urging me to let CBRE know how important these practices were to them.

The question is how mindfulness and yoga are integrated into office life. Rather than having an area dedicated to them, and to relaxation in general, it may be that encouraging an entire office to practice mindfulness or take part in a group yoga session is the answer.

Practicing together could also enhance employees' feelings of compassion towards each other. There is a growing body of research-based evidence that indicates both mindfulness and yoga practice enhance feelings of compassion.[13] The benefits of employees feeling compassionate towards one another might well encourage valuable qualities such as loyalty and teamwork.

Employees should, however, not feel obliged to practice mindfulness or yoga. Passionate advocates of these practices who are convinced of the benefits tend to gloss over the fact that they're not for everyone. Yoga is not recommended for certainhealth conditions.[14] There is a dark side to mindfulness which has yet to be fully explored.[15]

13   David Desteno, "The Kindness Cure," (2015, July, 21) https://www.theatlantic.com/health/archive/2015/07/mindfulness-meditation-empathy-compassion/398867/

14   William J. Broad, "How Yoga Can Wreck Your Body," (2012, January, 5) http://www.nytimes.com/2012/01/08/magazine/how-yoga-can-wreck-your-body.html (Accessed June, 6 2017)

15   Ruth Baer and Willem Kuyken, "Is Mindfulness Safe?" (2016, May, 23) https://www.mindful.org/is-mindfulness-safe/ (Accessed 18 June, 2017)

Of course, the solution to mitigating any potential risks is to work with accredited teachers. If employees recognize the benefits of the practices for themselves they can go deeper on their own time.

David, my co-writer, is very comfortable with practicing mindfulness and yoga and can step into this state easily. For people who struggle with mindfulness or yoga, like me, walking in a wooded or green area is a perfectly good alternative that can easily become routine.

While they clearly offer potentially enormous benefits to organizations and employees, mindfulness and yoga practice need to be integrated purposefully into office life to have measurable long-term benefits.

ACTIVE WORKDAYS

It's probably not surprising that everyone who took part in the research came to the conclusion that active spaces belong in the office. The healthy alternatives to chairs and the active conference room were used by 75% of participants for at least part of the day. Employees began to check in face to face with each other rather than send emails, although this was probably motivated more by the need to reach their 10,000-step daily goal than anything else.

Whatever the reason, employees did change their habits. They also perceived their work performance to be 10% improved.

Although we saw positive results, people did sometimes find it difficult to use some of the things we introduced while they were typing or writing. It turned out to be rather hard to use a treadmill at a desk. Only 12% of participants reported using treadmills at desks. However, medicine balls proved popular. All respondents (100%) used the exercise balls at some point and said they should become a permanent fixture. It did occur to us that if bicycles became a permanent feature in conference rooms, the speed at which a person paddled might become an indicator of how their mind was working as well as possibly become a distraction.

Just 12% participated in walking meetings. They seem to work best with small groups. Of course, weather conditions can also be a problem. Fortunately, our Active Workdays Month happened during the Dutch summer so the weather was mostly sunny. Those who did go on walking meetings told us that they were a great way of breaking up the day. Once again, we wondered if walking speed might become a factor in organizational politicking.

"The fact that your employer gives you the opportunity to relax, strengthens me to bring more mindfulness/relaxation into my work life. I have experience with the chair massage at my previous employer. I would recommend it strongly."

—*Participant, healthy offices research*

THE STATS

12%   improvement of measured performance

12%   improvement of self-rated performance

75%   used active spaces for part of the day

71%   felt healthier

69%   used the bike seat at their desk or meeting room

66%   said the bike seat should be included in the office

65%   felt more energized

36%   felt happier

Looking forward

We spend most of our waking lives at work and we're expected to perform at our best. Being physically active throughout the day is obviously good for our health, which is good for our performance and ultimately an organization's bottom line. But work in office environments has yet to evolve to a point where the right levels of steady, sensible activity are possible while people work.

Of course, there are potential problems. It's not hard to imagine people who are compulsive exercisers or obsessed with their weight prioritizing activity over doing their job properly. People who loathe exercise, especially if it's forced on them, may well put their valuable time and energy into avoiding it.

There is also the challenge of finding the sweet spot where someone is moving enough to feel the benefits but not so much that they lose concentration. Doctors have recommended getting up from a desk several times per hour. But how does someone actually do this without it affecting their work? At the same time, the potential benefits of incorporating steady, controlled physical activity into the office environments are enormous. To give one example, physical activity could be used to generate energy to power electronic devices and employees could earn rewards for this.

As with everything, it comes down to organizations being willing to put effort into creating the right kind of framework to truly benefit their people.

NATURAL SPACES

The amount of plant life, whether real or fake, in the CBRE office grew from minimal to having something in view of every workstation. We distributed full length wall murals and both real and fake plants throughout the healthy area. Murals were placed on a few large walls and in some flex offices and conference rooms. Plants were added to the center of work spaces and in eating areas. The results of our research certainly indicated the power of natural spaces. Employees who sat in the healthy spot rated their work performance to be 9% higher. Both real and fake plants had beneficial effects.

In addition to increased productivity, participants enjoyed the natural elements, stating that other areas of the building seemed dull in comparison.

"I was working and went to look out the window and realized I was looking at the mural. It was bizarre because I knew it wasn't real."
—Participant, *healthy offices research*

THE STATS

10%   improvement of measured performance

17%   improvement of self-rated performance

78%   feel happier

76%   felt more energized in the space

75%   preferred plants in the office

72%   found the workspace more comfortable

66%   like working in an environment that feels natural

65%   felt healthier

60%   felt more motivated

56%   like working in an office with wall art or plants

Looking forward

The German social psychologist, sociologist and psychoanalyst Erich Fromm coined the phrase "biophilia" to describe human "love of life or living systems."[16] He meant our psychological attraction to everything that is alive and vital. The notion of biophilia was popularized by Edward O. Wilson in his book of the same name. Wilson defines biophilia as "the urge to affiliate with other forms of life."

Biophilia is the reason why we relax when we hit the beach and drift off listening to the sound of the waves. It's why being around certain animals and coming into contact with them makes us feel good. And it's also why being in nature—for example, in a forest—is good for our mental and physical health.

Despite the fact that we're well aware of the benefits of being in nature, the limited extent to which plants and green spaces exist in offices indicates that we haven't considered the negative effects of being deprived of greenery, both physical and psychological.

16   *https://en.wikipedia.org/wiki/Biophilia_hypothesis*

HEALTHY LIGHTING

On the first day of our research participants struggled to get used to the lighting change. By the second day, however, they told us that they were very happy with it. After the month was over, participants that worked in the healthy spot, rated their work performance to be 18% higher during the month we changed the lighting. No one preferred the old lighting: 97% of participants didn't have a problem with glare, 95% liked the overall lighting and 89% liked the brightness.

When we changed the lighting in the office back to the old setting after the research was over people thought we'd actually turned the lights off. They asked to return to the lighting settings we'd used during the research.

The effect of changing lighting was as much of a revelation to me as it was for the people taking part in my research study.

"From the outside the light looks very unattractive. When you are sitting in the area it's very pleasant. The light becomes almost like daylight and kept me more alert."

—*Participant, healthy offices research*

THE STATS

12%   improvement of measured performance

18%   improvement in self-rated performance

87%   liked the light color

76%   felt happier

71%   felt more energetic

60%   felt more motivated

57%   felt more alert

50%   felt healthier

Looking forward

Today I have no doubt that creating a human centric office lighting environment that uses natural daylight as a template is crucial in helping people feel healthy and productive. The problem is that organizations are reluctant to install human centric lighting because it's expensive and consumes more energy than regular lighting. They're also not entirely convinced of the benefits. Perhaps the results of our research will help.

The potential for human centric lighting and circadian friendly days is enormous. Sophisticated human centric lighting systems integrated with technology that monitors individuals could, for instance, record how much natural daylight an employee has been exposed to and suggest they take a walk outside or move to a desk closer to a window. Or, offices could have glass ceilings that filtered out harmful rays and adjusted to different levels of brightness.

Whatever happens in the future, it's clear that typical lighting in offices today is not conducive to people being highly productive. Most office lighting is dimmer than natural daylight and is usually only positioned above our heads. This doesn't allow our eyes to absorb light effectively.

We need to consider the effects of knowledge workers (aka: office employees) sitting in an environment where lighting is, if not actually unhealthy, not delivering the benefits of natural daylight.

Most of all, our experiments with lighting proved that most offices today are highly unnatural environments in which to work. We still function best and feel best in natural light, in green areas, eating natural food and drinking water, being active and mindful.

PART FOUR

LOOKING FORWARD

Our research showed that physically active, mentally relaxed people who eat and drink in a healthy way perform better. To be honest, we would have been surprised if that wasn't the case. What took us by surprise was the way in which taking part in our research inspired people to change their lifestyles outside of work.

Using Deepak Chopra and Wouter's terminology, people "self repaired," and these changes extended to include their home and family lives..

This was partly due to the goal structure or gamified element of the wearable technology. Employees moved around more at work to try to achieve their goal of 10,000 steps. Before the research project started, I knew that this was a challenging number of steps but I also knew I needed to set the bar high. It turned out it was almost impossible to take 10,000 steps during week days—6,000 was about the limit. But employees could comfortably do 10,000 on weekend days and they did.

They also reduced their caffeine and sugar intake every day, not just at work, to have a better chance of getting eight hours of sleep. Over time, exercising and adjusting their behavior to move more and sleep better became a habit.

When we interviewed people who took part in the research after we'd finished, they told us that they'd also made changes to their homes and family lifestyles to make them healthier. In some instances, spouses and children took to the healthier lifestyle as well. One person told me that, instead of eating something sugary before an exam to get a rush, her child ate fruit instead. Apparently, the child's results were better than normal.

We were delighted that this was the case but our research was about the office environment. Remember that we spend on average a third of our waking week at work. Whatever changes are made within that environment are bound to affect us, perhaps profoundly. Organizations that embrace change have a great opportunity to improve the health of the people who are their most valuable assets, help ensure their longevity, attract the brightest and best and use their commitment to healthy office environments to differentiate themselves and create positive PR.

But let's also not forget the question of work-life balance. Talking with Dieter Lang, the lighting expert from Osram one day, he asked the question "Should we give our best hours to work?"

My instinctive response was "Of course." Then I started to think about it. I had assumed that the goal should always be for employees to be as productive and alert as possible when they're working. They can always relax and sleep at home. But inviting employees to relax and even sleep during those parts of the day when people naturally slow down a little—mid-afternoon, for instance—would help them to quite simply feel better physically and mentally. This might cause them to perform better on any given day but the real effect would be on their quality of life overall.

Organizations would benefit from enhanced employee performance but also because they would be seen as providing enlightened conditions in which to work. This could potentially enable employers to attract the radical workers they need.

Incidentally, Dieter asked his question after he'd just finished telling me that, in Europe, a perfect day in terms of the amount of light is the first of May, when the sun rises between 5:30 and 6 a.m. and sets at about 8 to 8:30 p.m.. The first of May is, appropriately enough, International Workers' Day, in many countries.

If workers are an organization's biggest asset, it makes absolute sense to do everything possible to provide an environment where their quality of life is at least as important a consideration as their productivity.

Who knows, they might even help enable real change in the wider world.

It seems highly likely that healthy offices can become catalysts for organizational change and not just at the individual level. The opportunity to work in a healthier environment within an ecosystem could easily become a privilege offered to valuable employees. Involving people in changing their own office environment by giving them the tools to make this happen would be especially empowering and, of course, reduce the cost an organization would have to bear itself.

But, the question is whether organizations will make the effort to change the way they view office environments and treat their people. Are they going to continue to drive people towards burnout, despite the fact that evidence points to the need to attract and keep the brightest, best "radical workers," as Wouter describes them? Even though they know people are their biggest investment, there is often the tendency for companies to focus on short rather than long term goals. I can't help but compare attitudes to climate change denial. It's obvious to most of us that we need to do something about climate change but we're not doing anywhere near enough. If organizations want to get the most out of their biggest resource, offices have to change, and soon. It's as simple as that.

There has to be a revolution.

SOME CONCLUSIONS

Epilogue

The Brits were only the first to be super-excited about what we were doing. Word spread throughout CBRE and pretty soon we were talking to offices all over Europe.

Today, Wouter and I, together with the CBRE team, are in the process of developing a consultancy approach that uses our research findings to persuade organizations to change the way they view their office ecosystems and their people. It's early, but we're getting a great response from the people we pitch the idea to. As Wouter predicted, the combination of research methods and the data gathered from wearable devices is nearly impossible to argue with.

The data collected at CBRE has gone to the University of Twente, where I am working on my PhD. We hope it's just the first stage in generating an enormous database of information about employee mental health in the Netherlands. I hadn't realized before I started, but there's actually very little research into "normal" working conditions. My findings are particularly valuable because the research was carried out in normal office conditions rather than extreme work settings such as night shift working or hospital emergency rooms.

Another benefit is that the study was done on the Dutch. These are some of the healthiest and happiest people in the world, yet their burnout rate is increasing. Perhaps this is the influence of the US, UK, and Japan. I hope to carry out comparative research in offices in different countries that will provide me with some answers.

And now I'm looking at a whole new career, consulting on work wellness. It would be a little too simple to say that I now have the opportunity to help other people avoid the sort of experience I had at The Agency, providing a neat resolution to my story. But it is kind of true. The damage I did to myself at The Agency, helped along by my naiveté about the environment I was working in, was finally mended by everything I learned and experienced at CBRE.

Nicholas—who you met earlier on in the book and who is now my husband—and I have set up Learn Adapt Build (LAB), a boutique agency combining real research with dramatic practical change. LAB works with companies on healthy offices, employee engagement, motivation and leadership. We facilitate change and improve workplaces. Our passion comes from experiencing the best and the worst in corporate environments as well as our desire to create change.

Now that I have some distance from my time with The Agency, I can honestly say I don't regret anything. I learned about how collaboration with the right person—usually your total opposite—really does lead to the kind of creativity you just can't achieve on your own. I'm also privileged to know what it's like to be really pushed to do good work to the point that, just when you think you can't do more, you discover that you can.

But I now know that if you're going to challenge people to perform to the limit of what they think they can achieve, go beyond this limit and surprise themselves, it's our duty to create a safe, healthy culture, and environment where the euphoria of accomplishment is accompanied by rest and rejuvenation.

The "rock and roll" culture of The Agency damaged me at the time. It didn't just affect my health. A negative philosophy regarding the importance of accomplishment above almost everything else became so deeply ingrained in me that it wasn't surprising I almost burned myself out all over again. I became immersed in a blind determination to complete a complex study and finish the research in time for the CoreNet conference. I could have told Wouter that it was too much or too soon, that I didn't have time and needed to modify the expectation as to what could be ready in time for the conference. After all, what difference would that have made in the overall context of my life and career? But, no, I pushed myself to meet a deadline with what could have resulted in negative consequences to my health.

This proved to me that burnout is like addiction: incredible highs followed by exhaustion, reduced productivity, and symptoms of depression. People who care and want to make a difference in the world are always potentially at risk of burning out, as well as those who are desperately trying to prove something, either to themselves or others. Put these people in a situation where their ambition, dedication and simple desire to do amazing work are triggered, and there's a danger they'll burn out over and over again. If the cause of an addiction is not identified and dealt with, a person will always be an addict, chasing after something ill-defined and potentially deadly. When I burned out at The Agency it was because my intense desire to do a great job collided with The Agency's culture of pushing people to the limit and beyond. We were perfect for each other in that way.

I'm so glad I didn't stay hidden away in the ivory tower of academia. My take on research is that it only counts for something if it can be applied in the real world to make people's lives better.

By turning my back on the work environment and going into academia, where of course there are still pressures, I was able to get some distance from work culture. But I clearly hadn't been able to make sense of why I worked the way I did.

As a woman in her mid-thirties I now understand myself more, so I was able to step back from burning out all over again. But what about the Millennial Generation and those that come after them? These are the people receiving mixed messages from society and from organizations: "You're too impatient and demand too much, but we want you to be independent-thinking radical workers who are creative and innovative. You're too dependent on technology, always looking at your smart phones, but we want you to be masters of technology. You're aware of your health, but we'll get you addicted to coffee and sugar—not for sinister reasons—but because stimulants are part of our culture, enabling us to ignore and push beyond exhaustion. You're socially aware and want to be the change in the world that you want to see. And we want to be seen as a socially conscious organization but not to the extent that it threatens our bottom line or any business that we do."

Right now, a generation is being made to hate itself, or at least to judge its worth on the basis of its accomplishments. Psychologists have found that the brain is wired for "effort driven reward." This causes us to seek measurable accomplishments as a source of satisfaction and self-esteem, making it even more difficult for us to step back and judge our worth on personal qualities such as perseverance (rather than success) or good collaborative skills (rather than being the one who gets the credit). I'm one of the oldest Millennials but this is my generation and I don't want us to be lost in the world of work. Not when there is so much to be excited about, so much potential for organizations to truly change the way they treat people and for people to be the change.

Not long after we settled on the title The Healthy Office Revolution, we realized it spelled out the acronym THOR. I'm proud of my Swedish origins and a diehard comic book fan so I loved the association with Norse mythology and superheroes. Better still, Thor is known for his strength, which he uses to protect humanity.

In my own small way, I have become stronger through the journey of doing my research and writing this book. My hope is that by writing about my experience I can play a part in protecting the health and wellbeing of the millions of people who work in offices every day. Most of all, I want to offer people information they simply can't unlearn.

Months after I presented my research findings, someone who'd been in the audience contacted me. They told me they couldn't get the data relating to how the brain is affected by healthy and unhealthy substances and environments out of their head (apologies for the pun). This had changed the way they worked.

I was thrilled by this. Not just from a scientific perspective but a human one. I'd shared information with someone and they couldn't unlearn it. Which meant they couldn't go back to their old ways of working. That person is a decision-maker in an organization.

And now it begins.

"So says THOR!"

The problem with so many books that criticize existing systems and conditions is that they fail to offer a workable alternative. One of the catalysts for this book was a conversation that I had with David, my co-writer, about Dave Eggers's 2013 book *The Circle*, now a movie.

At the time we were working together on a digital health blog. David was—and is—as fascinated by the potential of wearables as I am. He's also deeply immersed in yoga and teaches it to enhance a writing practice so he's constantly exploring the connections between the mind and body. But he's far warier than I am when it comes to organizations and their motives. And he loathes offices. Which is why he's worked as a digital nomad for just about all of his working life.

If you don't already know, *The Circle* is the story of Mae Holland, a young Californian "everywoman," and what happens to her when she joins the largest hi-tech firm in the world. The organization, called The Circle, is obviously inspired by Google, Facebook and any other Silicon Valley giant you care to mention. In an interview, Eggers said, "A lot of times I'd think of something that a company like The Circle might dream up, something a little creepy, and then I'd read about the exact invention, or even something more extreme, the next day."[17]

We both loved the book. But for different reasons. Although I knew it was dark and dystopian, I was drawn to the descriptions of the Circle's campus-style office and the sense of community created within the workplace. I understood why Mae, the central character, loved the Circle.

There's an ancient, intrinsic drive in all of us to belong to a tribe or community. For many of us, this is our workplace. We spend most of our waking and sometimes most rewarding hours with our colleagues. Our work gives us a clearly defined role and purpose, as well as opportunities for socializing. The bond can become extremely powerful. This is why being fired or "let go" and then escorted out on the same day you receive the news is such a cruel and unusual punishment. You've been excommunicated. Your sense of purpose vanishes in an instant. You no longer belong. And you don't even get to say good bye.

David relished Eggers's attack on Silicon Valley and the tech behemoths. He freely admits to being deeply cynical about business and corporations and believes that organizations are motivated entirely by their bottom line.

At one point in our conversation about the book, David said, "What I find interesting is that everything I find disturbing you like."

This was born out in the real world when we discussed a visit I made to "opportunity space" Epicenter in Stockholm. About itself, Epicenter says "We offer space for people and organizations to work, co-work and exchange ideas and creative energy with other entrepreneurs, start-ups and big global names. There are studios, silent zones and creative spaces. We have an

17   "A Brief Q&A with Dave Eggers about **The Circle**." https://www.mcsweeneys.net/pages/a-brief-q-a-with-dave-eggers-about-the-circle (Accessed 18 June, 2017)

excellent restaurant offering delicious healthy, nutritional food and drink."

People who use Epicenter, its members, are invited to have a radio-frequency identification (RFID) chip about the size of a grain of rice embedded in their hand. The logic is that they don't have to carry around swipe cards, that could get lost, or use cash to pay for things like lunch. They also don't have to remember so many passwords or pin codes. The chips enable members to open doors, activate photocopiers or pay in the Epicenter restaurant just by touching their hand.

When we interviewed Liselotte Appel at Epicenter, she told us "It's all part of our belief that the future lies in the humanization of technology. We live in fantastic times, don't we? When disabled people can wear suits that enable them to walk. We want to be part of this."

I couldn't agree more. I loved the idea of the chip. It absolutely horrified David. He saw the chip as potentially a profound invasion of his privacy. When we discussed our feelings, however, we did agree that it all comes down to ethics. In a talk he gave at Stanford University, Eggers said, "People will do the right thing when there are laws and parameters and when there's a discussion about it." He added, "I'm a believer. I believe we're good. We just need to talk about how to be good."

Although David and I were, and sometimes still are, polar opposites in our attitudes towards organizations, we agreed with Eggers. Technology is hugely beneficial in the office environment as long as it's governed by a code of ethics.

Given that this is the case, allow me to share my own vision of a utopian office, an offitopia.

I would start with the office environment itself. There would be plenty of well-kept plant life to reduce carbon dioxide in the air as well as stress. There might even be a garden where we could grow food, including the herbs for our drinks. Employees would be encouraged to work in the garden for exercise and also as a form of relaxation. The garden would also be a space for mindfulness and perhaps yoga. Produce grown in the garden would be used for healthy meals and snacks.

The office itself would have a natural flow to it. There would be plenty of space to allow people to walk around whenever they felt like it. The main staircase would be a central feature—research shows that people are far more likely to use the stairs if a staircase is open and beautifully designed.

My offitopia would have as much flexible working space as possible, reflecting the changing emphasis of work from desk to project-based. Flexible working spaces would also enable people to interact with each other, helping to create more of a collaborative community that supported people with tools and technology and inspired people to do their best work. However, many spaces would be private or quiet for individual work.

What hours they worked would be, within reason, up to them. My research proved to me that we don't all work best at the same time of day. For some people, a nine to five is a cruel and unnatural punishment. For others, an all-nighter is traumatic.

People in my offitopia would be judged on output and incentivized to work in a way that's both productive and healthy. Managers would be trained to help support and empower employees, based on their output. They would be educated on the dangers of stress and fear based management on work quality. Right now, many mangers only evaluate their employees by seeing how much time they spend at their desks. However, encouraging managers to know exactly what their employees are working on and whether they're meeting their goals, without simply checking whether they're at their desks or not is key to output-based-management.

There might also be a campus-style element to my offitopia. I'm married and at the time of writing, expecting my first baby, so my days of wanting to be part of a Millennial gang are gone. But, in principle, I see the appeal with living and working campus-style. Especially if my offitopia was in an expensive city like San Francisco, London or Stockholm. I would be pleased if I could offer subsidized, affordable homes to young people while they were getting on their feet.

If young, ambitious people came home to a well-designed apartment they shared with people they already knew from work, they would hopefully be in an environment where they and their triggers for burnout were understood. This could help prevent them from burning out or becoming isolated.

Technology would, of course, underpin everything. I understand, and to a certain extent, share David's reservations about technology and data collection. But my research project demonstrated how valuable wearables, beacons, and the data they gather can be. In my offitopia, technology would only be used in a way that benefits employees as much as it does the people gathering the data. The focus would be on health and working smarter. Nothing more.

Completing the circle: why healthy? why wearable technology? why me?

I started my research into healthy offices because I believed I could prove that the performance of our brains and bodies can be enhanced by technology as well as environment. In the process of writing this book I realized that the real reason was rooted in my own experience. This was why I fought so hard to make my research project happen.

People often believe that I must be a techie but I'm not. I'm no early adopter and I have no idea what the coolest new technology is. I love technology for the same reason I love super-heroes and Norse gods. It has amazing power to do good and how we react to it says something about us. I know this from firsthand experience.

When I was seventeen I was a passenger in a car that was involved in a bad car crash. The car flipped over and I ended up with a battered body, skull fracture, and bruising in my brain. I was eventually stabilized and discharged from the hospital but I had memory loss, concentration problems, and trouble reading. I also had really intense and inappropriate emotional reactions to situations as well as constant, severe headaches. The narcotics they gave me for pain seemed to make my emotions worse, causing me to choose the pain and reject the medications. These intense emotional reactions diminished slightly but continued even after I stopped taking the narcotics. One of the areas of injury to my brain was in the right frontal lobe, which has something to do with emotional control.

It was so serious that my doctors wanted to send me to a long-term rehabilitation facility that helped people with brain injuries get used to their new lives. I heard awful rumors that they hung a notebook around a patient's neck with their address on it and taught them to write down everything they needed to remember.

The thought of living at home for the rest of my life without a memory, unable to control my emotions or read absolutely terrified me. Being helpless and unable to pursue my dreams was unacceptable.

But I was incredibly lucky. At the time of my accident my mom was a psychologist working with the court system and she'd been researching the possibility of treating brain injury and other problems such as ADHD and depression with EEG biofeedback technologies. She was working with the brilliant John K. Nash and used me as a guinea pig as well as her research assistant. It was fascinating for both of us. This meant referring me to a neuropsychologist who treated people with a variety of technologies that included EEG biofeedback and vision therapy. My mom had a record of my mental performance levels before the accident as a target for us to reach.

When I got out of the hospital we began working on my brain therapy almost right away. The neuropsychologist first gave me a Quantitative EEG, which measured what was happening in my brain when I performed certain tasks such as reading. Then I had therapy to correct the problem. A sensor was placed on my scalp in the area that was identified as causing the problem and the computer was programmed to reward me when my brain did the right thing. For example, I was "rewarded" by musical tones or when the hot air balloon on the computer screen flew into the target zone. That meant that my brain was correcting the problem. The neuropsychologist called this brain exercise, stressing that the brain was a muscle. I learned what to do to make my brain focus and function normally. After a while it happened all by itself and I didn't need the therapy sessions or the machinery any more.

Reading was an especially serious problem because it caused severe headaches. I learned that this is a common problem for people after head injuries. Each eye sees something in a slightly different place, so I had double vision and my eyes had to work very hard to focus. It turned out that the reason I couldn't read had something to do with my brain as well as my eyes so I had to treat both to fix the problem. Since my eyes weren't properly focusing, reading gave me blurry vision almost immediately and this was followed by agonizing headaches and exhaustion. At each session of EEG biofeedback I also practiced focusing my eyes with a series of exercises that the doctor said were about convergence and divergence. After my eyes were trained, I worked on my speed reading and I'm now able to get through material incredibly quickly—invaluable for a researcher.

The next thing was working on my emotions and, again, the sensor/sensors were placed on the parts of my brain that had been injured and that were causing my intense emotions. I practiced suppressing the brain waves that were causing the problems and creating calming (slower) brain waves. Interestingly enough, some of the brain waves the machinery taught me to generate are at the same slow speed of a person who is high on marijuana.

It was such a relief when I started to get back my composure, like becoming me again. As my brain got back to normal, something was switched on in me. My mom and I continued treatment way past what was necessary and my scores soared far beyond what I had done before the accident.

I decided I'd never give up on anything that mattered to me ever again. I never have. It became my dream to get my PhD.

My experience of working at The Agency was the other factor that decided the direction in which my research would go, although this didn't occur to me until afterwards. When I began, all I knew was that academics were excited about the possibilities of introducing wearable technology into the workplace. Pretty much all of the thinking was around using wearables to simply monitor employee performance and health. I realized that no one was looking at wearables as a way to change office environments and enable people to become more productive in a way that increases their long-term value to the company.

Obviously, I was looking to the future—my career as much as the world of work itself. But I finally understood towards the end of writing this book that I wanted to offer the missing pieces to organizations like The Agency that would enable them to tap into their employees' greatest potential by creating truly healthy working environments.

I was, and am, on a mission.

Elizabeth Nelson and David Holzer July 2017